D1365962

Va

Screen

Vampire Lovers

Screen's Seductive Creatures of the Night

a book of undead pin-ups

Gavin Baddeley

Plexus, London

Copyright © 2010 by Plexus Publishing Limited
Published by Plexus Publishing Limited
25 Mallinson Road
London SW11 1BW
www.plexusbooks.com

British Library Cataloguing in Publication Data

Baddeley, Gavin.
    Vampire lovers : screen's seductive creatures of the night.
    1. Vampire films--History and criticism.
    I. Title
    791.4'3675-dc22

    ISBN-13: 978-0-85965-450-0
    ISBN-10: 0-85965-450-8

Cover and book design by Coco Wake-Porter
Printed in Great Britain by Scotprint

Acknowledgements

Thanks to Laura Coulman, my editor at Plexus, for her
insightful editorial assistance and expertise on all things
undead; to my book designer, Coco Wake-Porter, for creating
the look; and above all to my very own creature of the night,
Keri, who helped on so many levels. Thanks also to Salvation
Films and Fab Press. – *Gavin Baddeley*

We would like to thank the following for supplying
photographs: *Twilight:* Everett Collection/ Rex Features/
Summit Entertainment; *True Blood:* Your Face Goes Here
Entertainment/ HBO; Gavin Baddeley Archive/Your Face
Goes Here Entertainment/ HBO; *The Vampire Diaries:* C.CW
Network/ Everett/ Rex Features; *Being Human:* Victoria
Ramirez, RDF Rights, RDF Media Group; *Van Helsing:*
Moviestore Collection/ Universal Pictures; *Underworld:*
Lakeshore Entertainment; *Angel:* Kuzui Entertainment/ 20th
Century Fox Television; *Razor Blade Smile:* Gavin Baddeley
Archive/ Palm Pictures; *Buffy The Vampire Slayer:* Mutant
Enemy/ 20th Century Fox Television; *From Dusk Till Dawn:*
Dimension Films/ Miramax; *Interview with the Vampire:*
Moviestore Collection/ Geffen Pictures/ Warner Bros; BFI
Stills, Posters and Designs/ Warner Bros/ Geffen Pictures;
Bram Stoker's Dracula: American Zoetrope/ Columbia;
Innocent Blood: Moviestore Collection/ Warner Bros; *The
Lost Boys:* Warner Bros; Gavin Baddeley Archive/ Warner
Bros; *Vamp:* Gavin Baddeley Archive/ Balcor Film Investors/
Planet Productions; *Dracula:* Universal Pictures; Moviestore
Collection/ Universal Pictures; Gavin Baddeley Archive/
Universal Pictures; *Blood for Dracula:* Gavin Baddeley Archive/
Compagnia Cinematografica Champion; *Blacula:* Gavin
Baddeley Archive/ American International Pictures; Gavin
Baddeley Archive/ Compagnia Cinematografica Champion;
Daughters of Darkness: Gavin Baddeley Archive/ Showking
Films; *Vampire Lovers:* AIP/ Hammer Film Productions; Plexus
Archive/ AIP/ Hammer Film Productions; Gavin Baddeley
Archive/AIP/ Hammer Film Productions; *Dark Shadows:*
Dan Curtis Productions; *Dracula: Prince of Darkness:* Gavin
Baddeley Archive/ Hammer Film Productions; Hammer Film
Productions; *Black Sunday:* Gavin Baddeley Archive/ Altavista
Productions; *Horror of Dracula:* Hammer Film Productions;
Gavin Baddeley Archive/ Hammer Film Productions; *Dracula's
Daughter:* Gavin Baddeley Archive/ Universal Pictures; *Dracula:*
Universal Pictures; Gavin Baddeley Archive/ Universal Pictures.

    We would like to thank the following film production
companies and distributors: Summit Entertainment; Your
Face Goes Here Entertainment; HBO; C.CW Network; RDF
Rights, RDF Media Group; Universal Pictures; Lakeshore
Entertainment; Kuzui Entertainment/ 20th Century Fox
Television; Palm Pictures; Mutant Enemy/ 20th Century Fox
Television; Dimension Films/ Miramax; Geffen Pictures/
Warner Bros; American Zoetrope/ Columbia; Warner Bros;
Warner Bros; Balcor Film Investors/ Planet Productions;
Universal Pictures; Compagnia Cinematografica Champion;
American International Pictures; Compagnia Cinematografica
Champion; Showking Films; AIP/ Hammer Film Productions;
Dan Curtis Productions; Altavista Productions; Hammer Film
Productions; Universal Pictures.

Contents

Introduction

'Whether you come from heaven or hell, what does it matter, O Beauty!'

Vampirism is all about sex. It's a contentious assertion you'll find in the first few pages of pretty much every book on the vampire myth published over the past 50 years or so; an idea that is now so familiar – such a statement of the obvious – that it's practically redundant. As the title of the book you're currently holding suggests, it's not one we're about to argue with here: our focus is upon the vampire as a screen sex symbol. But it is worth noting that the vision of the vampire as an essentially sexual entity is a comparatively new one, far from universally accepted even today. (Writer Steve Niles deliberately went against the trend for romantic bloodsuckers in his 2007 film *30 Days of Night*. 'My vampires don't care at all about seduction,' he said. 'It's all about food to them.') The reports of strange events in Eastern Europe that first introduced the word 'vampire' into the English language in the mid-1700s described creatures very different to the suave creatures of the night we're familiar with today. The undead of authentic folklore were smelly, bloated, purple-faced peasants; not elegant, pale and interesting aristocrats.

The transformation of the vampire, from the repulsive walking cadaver that filled our distant ancestors with dread, to the dark romantic fantasy figure that thrills us on the screen today, was a gradual one. It began in the Gothic novels, popular melodramas and romantic verse of the 1800s, gaining pace as the undead adapted to the new media of film and television in the twentieth century. The Parisian poet Charles Baudelaire was instrumental in reinventing the vampire as a symbol of poisonous sexual desire, most notably in his highly controversial, but equally influential 1857 volume of verse, *Les Fleurs du Mal,* or 'The Flowers of Evil'. (The quotes employed in this introduction are taken from the decadent pen of Monsieur Baudelaire.) When the Anglo-Irish author Bram Stoker created the immortal vampire Count in his 1897 novel, *Dracula*, he had no intention of unleashing a sex demon. Yet many critics now agree that Dracula fed upon repressed Victorian sexuality just as greedily as he did human blood, a fictional monster who embodied forbidden desires such as no decent gentleman (like Bram) could ever have entertained – consciously, at least.

Most early screen vampires were nightmare manifestations rather than dreamboats. The celebrated 1922 silent German film *Nosferatu* featured a bald bloodsucker, played by

Max Schreck (whose surname translates as 'dread'), who resembled a cross between an emaciated corpse and a skinned rat. A decade later, in *Vampyr*, the noted Danish director Carl Dreyer imagined his supernatural predator as a ghostly crone. In Hollywood, however, the tide had already begun to turn the previous year with the release of *Dracula*, whose tuxedo-clad Count, played by Bela Lugosi, was cinema's first undead sex symbol. This is where our story begins.

Or, more accurately, ends. For in the following pages we take a chronological journey through the annals of screen vampirism in reverse, beginning with the most recent manifestations, and tracing the origin of the species through a succession of profiles. Inevitably, during this book's composition, many notable bloodsuckers have fallen by the wayside. If one of your personal favourites doesn't feature in the following pages, I can only apologise, offering some insight into the selection process by way of explanation. For *Vampire Lovers* I have endeavoured to gather a cast of vampires who will provide both a good guide to the evolution of the undead sex symbol and an idea of the wide variety of bloodsuckers who have given audiences deliciously bad (even wet) dreams over the past seven decades. Some are so popular that to even consider their exclusion was unthinkable. Others enjoy a more limited, cult appeal, but serve as colourful examples of the weird and wonderful forms the myth's erotic aspect has taken on when interpreted by maverick moviemakers from around the world. In each case, we try to pin down just what makes each individual vampire unique in their appeal, on occasion noting similar or related creatures of the night, worthy of attention as potential competition for the 'official candidate'.

By no means is every movie featured in this book a classic – or even necessarily a good film – but every bloodsucker we examine broke a few mortal hearts among the audience or signalled a new direction in the evolution of the archetype of the vampire lover. This survey confines itself to the screen. Initially, limiting the book's scope to cinematic vampires was also considered, but this would have left too much of the story untold. *Dark Shadows* made a huge impact on many young fans during its extensive run in the '60s. What would vampire culture have been in the '90s without *Buffy the Vampire Slayer* and its sundry spin-offs? Most recently, *True Blood* has been setting pulses racing with a steamy saga featuring the kind of explicit sex and brutal bloodshed previously confined to the big screen. In the US, TV drama has come of age in the wake of shows like *The Sopranos* (which debuted in 1999) featuring adult themes and content once unthinkable in the medium, and it seemed only right to reflect that by including small-screen vampires in our evaluation.

'The unique and supreme voluptuousness of love lies in the certainty of committing evil. And men and women know from birth that in evil is found all sensual delight.'

The main trend affecting the undead outside of television and cinema of late has been the advent of paranormal romance literature, which blends the traditional love story with supernatural elements. Some might argue that you can trace the genre's roots back to Anne Rice's *Vampire Chronicles*, beginning in 1976, or further still to the very roots of the Gothic novel in the late eighteenth century. As an identifiable genre, however, it is only in recent years that paranormal romance has become a true phenomenon, elbowing horror novels from their perch in many bookshop displays. *True Blood* owes its inspiration to *The Southern Vampire Mysteries*, a series of paranormal romance novels penned by Charlaine Harris, first published in 2001. If nothing else, the twenty-first-century rise of the vampire as a cliché in traditional romance fiction illustrates how far we have come from the repellent, malodorous undead parasite of 250 years ago.

In the eyes of some fang fans, we have come too far. For them, wholly divorcing the vampire from its undead roots – effectively humanising it – deprives the archetype of danger, destroying it even more surely than if you thrust a stake through its undead heart. Most such arguments centre around the popularity of *The Twilight Saga*, which began as a series of paranormal romance novels by the Mormon authoress Stephenie Meyer in 2005, leading to an equally successful film franchise three years later and now representing a phenomenon in its own right. Since I began researching and writing this book, it seems like practically every publication imaginable has run a 'top vampire' poll or survey of some description (a number of which are referenced). While they vary in quality and relevance, you can guarantee that few of these features would have seen the light of day without the *Twilight* phenomenon. Love it or loathe it, you cannot ignore this most divisive vampire romance.

Vampire Lovers aims to be both provocative and wide-ranging in its exploration of the most fascinating erotic archetype to haunt modern media. For those new to the vampire genre, I hope your eyes are opened to some undiscovered Gothic delights well worth beckoning over the threshold (or at least sliding into your DVD player). Equally, I trust veterans will find some of the analyses of old favourites and new contenders for the crown of prince (or princess) of darkness enlightening and engaging. I have watched (or in most cases re-watched) countless hours of undead TV and cinema (a pleasure rather than a duty, admittedly) and trawled through my archives to locate the most astute and intriguing commentaries on our subject. We begin each profile with a tagline – the promotional slogan used to sell the film – while peppering them with quotes from the vampire in question. In each, we try to get beneath the skin of our bloodsucker – the character, the actor, the production – in an effort to unveil the essence of why we find such creatures irresistible. In the process of lifting the coffin lid on our culture's creepiest fantasy figures, we will perhaps glimpse a few of the darker secrets of our own sexual identities.

'Enter freely and of your own will...'

Twilight

Robert Pattinson as Edward Cullen in *Twilight*

'When you can live forever, what do you live for?'

A taciturn high-school student in the rainy backwater town of Forks, Washington, Edward does little to draw attention to himself. Though he can't help but be the subject of a little local gossip… mostly because he's one of the Cullens, a family of ethereal stunners with strange topaz eyes and a long, secret history. The Cullen kids are seen as a little aloof by their fellow students. 'That's Edward Cullen,' observes classmate Jessica. 'He's totally gorgeous, obviously. But apparently, nobody here's good enough for him – like I care.' With his perfect, marble-pale complexion, distinctive carefully-tousled hair and striking, chiselled good looks – resembling nothing so much as a Classical statue – Edward can't help but stand out from his fellow students. But, conservatively dressed, polite and quietly spoken, Edward Cullen goes out of his way to keep himself to himself.

Robert Pattinson, the actor who plays Edward in the 2008 film *Twilight*, thinks that enigmatic self-absorption is the key to his character's appeal. 'It's being unreadable,' he says. 'It's attractive in women as well, just that kind of mystique. It's so obvious, but so few people do have it, especially in characters now and especially in modern society where there's so many celebrities.' Of course, Edward's angelic, faraway looks and his clan's cagey demeanour conceal a secret. The Cullens are not a regular family unit, but a vampire coven, presided over by the town doctor, Carlisle Cullen. Dr Cullen is a bloodsucker with a conscience, insisting his brood feed only on animals. Edward is an adoptive son any parent would be proud of – his impeccable manners and studious attitude twinned with just a hint of inner torment – so it's no surprise when Bella, the newest student at Forks High School, falls for him.

Kristen Stewart plays Bella, the sensible, slightly awkward teenager who finds her ambivalence towards the enigmatic Edward turning into something more than a crush. It's a building passion both of them soon struggle to control, compounded when Edward's supernatural secret is revealed, creating problems beyond those faced by most teen couples (even if Edward has remained a teenager since 1918). So, what's not to like about this romance between the softly-spoken vampire and the fresh-faced young Bella?

Robert Pattinson as conflicted vegetarian vampire, Edward Cullen.

For, strange to say, *Twilight* is probably the most controversial film to feature in this book. Odd, when these pages contain so many movies that broach the darkest reaches of the torrid territory where sex and death collide.

Yet amidst the wave of gratuitous celluloid bloodshed and big-screen sexual deviance to be found in the realms of vampire cinema, it is a film mild enough to warrant a '12' certificate that has inspired the most fervent controversy. In part it is this very restraint – the conspicuous absence of geysers of plasma or sweaty sexuality – which both allowed such a certificate and lies at the heart of the *Twilight* phenomenon. It was also instrumental in triggering such a vocal and visceral response in the vampire fan community. You also can't overlook the fact that *Twilight* is unquestionably both a commercial and cultural phenomenon. Something that inspires such deep and widespread devotion among so many dedicated fans always has the capacity to trigger an equal and opposite reaction among sceptics.

My family, we're different from others of our kind. We only hunt animals. We've learned to control our thirst. As to you, your scent – it's like a drug to me. You're like my own personal brand of heroin.'

In such a climate of fervent adoration and bitter backlash it becomes difficult to take a dispassionate view on *Twilight*; to separate the film and Robert Pattinson's performance in it from the deafening debate that surrounds both them and the original Stephenie Meyer novel from which they are derived… difficult and, perhaps, counterproductive. *Twilight* clearly touched a nerve, among both fans and opponents (and, at the risk of overstating the point, it's hard to think of another vampire film where you might refer to critics as 'opponents' of the movie). Dissecting this response helps us get closer to the character of Edward Cullen, helping the uninitiated understand why, as played by Robert Pattinson, he has become the pre-eminent undead pin-up on so many walls. Of course *Twilight* first became an overnight sensation as a book, when the novel was released as the first in a four-book *Saga* in 2005, introducing the world to Edward Cullen.

Edward was cast with some care. The film rights for *Twilight* had been snapped up by MTV films before the book had even been published. But the huge success of Stephenie Meyer's novel inspired a rethink and the project passed to Summit Entertainment in 2007, with a new script that stuck far closer to the original story and a greater role for the authoress herself in the creative process. Reports suggest that over 5,000 actors auditioned before Summit finally settled upon English actor Robert Pattinson for the part (Stephenie had originally envisaged Henry Cavill, another Englishman, as Edward). It was, perhaps, inevitable that the role of the sublimely beautiful vampire would go to a male model. 'I always looked like a girl up until a few years ago and because I never did any sports or anything, I was always kind of gangly,' says Robert. 'I was never really a good model. I was terrible at it.'

Edward endeavours to resist the temptation of Bella (Kristen Stewart).

In *Twilight* Edward Cullen has a somewhat androgynous appearance, in keeping with ever-changing viewer tastes. Indeed, girlish good looks have become a trend among male pin-ups over the past few decades. Starting, perhaps, with Glam-pop superstars like Marc Bolan and David Bowie in the '70s, via delicate-featured film stars such as Leonardo DiCaprio in more recent years, idols with more feminine features have enjoyed increasing popularity – particularly among younger female fans, who find the traditional, square-jawed macho-man intimidating and crass. Perhaps *Twilight* represents the furthest progression along similar lines within the realms of vampire cinema. Certainly, as we'll see later in these pages, while the undead Counts of yesteryear were seldom macho-men in the traditional mould, they were certainly masculine, while a tendency towards more sexually ambivalent bloodsuckers has developed over the decades.

Having said which, once Robert Pattinson had secured the lead in *Twilight*, he flew to the US, not just to perfect his American accent and obtain a local driving license, but also to undertake a punishing routine of physical training, in preparation for the demanding stunts, fight scenes and, indeed, the vampire baseball game featured in the script. While he had to look outwardly sensitive and delicate, Edward also had to be able to project intimidating power when the situation demanded it. This kind of contradictory appeal – of a gentle, even angelic character, tormented by the instincts of a bloodthirsty killer – goes some way towards explaining why Bella, the mortal girl played by Kristen Stewart, is so drawn to Edward.

Perhaps it's the same paradox, of a cherubic, tender monster, of beauty taming the beast that *Twilight* fans find so irresistible? 'That's exactly what it is,' Robert confirmed in an interview with *Rolling Stone* magazine. 'It's a certain type of girl. I don't know what it is – when you look at fan sites [you can tell] – but there's definitely a very large fleet of people, it's actually Americans, that want those type of guys. In the book she knows the whole time [that he's not going to hurt her], but Kristen and I tried to make it more not caring, more unpredictable. It's what I liked about the story – he's literally holding himself back [at] every single turn, never lets up. He's such a sort of gentlemanly character, and Kristen and I really, really emphasised that – especially when there are intimate scenes.' If anything, the actor observes, the film makes that conflict in his character, between Edward's supernatural bloodlust and his protective passion for Bella, more pronounced.

That conflict reaches a crescendo at the film's action-packed climax and, according to Pattinson, 'people who read the books won't be expecting it and, for a younger person's film, it's also quite shocking. When I read that scene in the book I thought it was kind of sexy and then when you translate it onto film, the kissing is a little like a thing out of a TV series. So I thought, "How can we make this thing a little bit on the verge of wrong?" … Edward's constantly saying, "I'm a monster, I'm a monster, I'm a monster," and doesn't end up being one. We shot the final scene first and I wanted the fight to not just be a fight, but to literally have him turn into that monster. In the book he very much comes in to save the day as the hero, but I noticed when we were doing the blocking it's the first time he's seen a lot of her blood – and I thought it would be interesting [for him to start] wanting to kill [Bella] and then fighting himself for that.'

Subsequent to Twilight, *Pattinson won numerous polls as a sex symbol and fan favourite.*

Despite this, for many of its critics, *Twilight* fell short because Edward wasn't enough of a monster, but rather an anaemic teen dream lacking any real bite. Similarly, some felt that Bella was too bland, that her story reads more like empty wish-fulfilment than carefully crafted plotting, reflecting none of the difficult times most adolescents go through in real life. The separation of her parents is notably amicable; the transition to her new school trouble-free. Even the vampire she meets turns out to be an Adonis with old-fashioned manners who wants nothing more than to protect her. In short, everything in the 'Twi-verse' seems a little too nice. In her defence, the authoress – a member of the Mormon faith – insists that much of the 'niceness' of her novels reflects her own personal experience. 'I grew up in a community where it was not the exception to be a good girl,' she says. 'It was sort of expected. And all of my friends were good girls too and my boyfriends were good boys. Everybody was pretty nice. And that affects how I write my characters. There aren't very many bad guys in my novels. Even the bad guys usually have a pretty good reason for the way they are and some of them come around in the end. I don't see the world as full of negatives.'

Twilight's theme – of innocent love in a vampiric context – divided critics and fans.

'You don't know how long I've waited for you...
And so the lion fell in love with the lamb.'

The strongest reaction against Stephenie Meyer's novels and the subsequent cinematic adaptations has come from within horror fandom. To the minds of many staunch aficionados, *Twilight* and its fang-free vampires – who sparkle rather than disintegrate in sunlight – are an insult to the whole genre, with its traditions of deviance and darkness. For her part, Stephenie points out that she's never claimed to be a horror novelist, or indeed had any particular interest in vampires outside of her own fiction. 'I've seen little pieces of *Interview with the Vampire* when it was on TV, but I kind of always go, "*YUCK!*"' she says. 'I don't watch R-rated movies, so that really cuts down on a lot of the horror. And I think I've seen a couple of pieces of *The Lost Boys*, which my husband liked and he wanted me to watch it once, but I was like, "It's creepy!"' She hasn't yet read

Stephen King helped revive the vampire genre in 1975 with his novel *'Salem's Lot* (adapted for TV in 1979 and 2004) which, like *Twilight*, successfully relocated the legend to contemporary small-town America. Kurt Barlow, the vampire in *'Salem's Lot*, is almost the direct opposite of Edward Cullen – a brutal, unrepentant monster who happily victimises children. (The memorable depiction of Barlow in the 1975 adaptation goes even further, presenting the vampire as a repulsive, inhuman ghoul with rodentine teeth; only his unnaturally golden eyes hint at any connection with the likes of Edward Cullen.) King invited controversy with some frank views on Stephenie Meyer's work made to *USA Weekend* in 2009. Meyer has frequently been compared to J.K. Rowling, whose *Harry Potter* books have proven hugely popular, transcending their younger target audience to enjoy popularity with readers of all ages. King recognised some parallels between the two authors – both were 'speaking directly to young people', he acknowledged. 'The real difference is that Jo Rowling is a terrific writer and Stephenie Meyer can't write worth a darn. She's not very good,' he added.

Inevitably, his comments inspired outrage among *Twilight* fans. Some insisted King was piqued by old-fashioned jealousy. Stephenie's novels have sold some 85 million copies worldwide, her success propelling her onto prestigious lists of the most influential and powerful celebrities today. Yet King's comments are worth repeating, as they contain at least a germ of truth, even if you don't endorse his dismal assessment of Meyer's writing skills. 'People are attracted by the stories,' he observed, 'by the pace and in the case of Stephenie Meyer, it's very clear that she's writing to a whole generation of girls and opening up kind of a safe joining of love and sex in those books. It's very exciting and it's thrilling and it's not particularly threatening because they're not overtly sexual. A lot of the physical side of it is conveyed in things like the vampire will touch her forearm or run a hand over skin, and she just flushes all hot and cold. And for girls, that's a shorthand for all the feelings that they're not ready to deal with yet.'

Part of *Twilight*'s appeal rests in its innocence – a story where the tension of sexual abstinence actually amplifies the erotic tension between the vampire and his willing victim. 'I get some pressure to put a big sex scene in,' says Meyer. 'But you can go anywhere for graphic sex. It's harder to find a romance where they dwell on the handholding. I was a late bloomer. When I was sixteen, holding hands was just – wow.' The more chaste tone of the *Twilight* books and movies has also broadened their appeal – both to older readers who appreciate supernatural thrills that don't hinge upon graphic sex or violence and younger fans who might find the more overtly erotic character of more adult vampire fantasies 'YUCK' or 'creepy'. 'It's weird that you get eight-year-old girls coming up to you saying, "Can you just bite me? I want you to bite me,"' observes Robert Pattinson of the more bizarre aspects of his new star status. 'It is really strange how young the girls are, considering the book is based on the virtues of chastity, but I think it has the opposite

Robert Pattinson as Edward Cullen in *Twilight*

True Blood

Alexander Skarsgård as Eric Northman in *True Blood*

'Thou shall not crave thy neighbour.'

With *True Blood*, some might argue that the screen vampire finally came of age. There have been X-rated undead flicks aplenty, and smash hit teen-orientated TV serials, but the 2008 HBO series has broken new ground by penetrating the commercial and critical mainstream, while truly going for the jugular with adult content that would have been unthinkable on a TV show in years gone by. In response to an interviewer who suggested that the sex scenes were 'ballsy', the show's star Stephen Moyer responded, 'If you look very closely on one of the wide shots, it's *very* ballsy!' *True Blood* goes beyond sexual daring, however, to address such challenging issues as drugs and prejudice, using the vampire metaphor to explore the horrors of addiction and racism in all of their troubling complexity. When the invention of synthetic blood allows vampires to come 'out of the coffin' and integrate into 'regular' society, the amorality of the vampire lays bare much human immorality. Most importantly for ratings figures, perhaps, *True Blood* has an iconic vampire lead in Stephen Moyer as the tall, dark and handsome gentleman bloodsucker Bill Compton.

Which begs the question, why head our profile with Eric Northman, the blonde Scandinavian vampire played by Alexander Skarsgård? It's a judgement call likely to make more than one *True Blood* devotee, well, spit blood. It's also a debate worth exploring, opening up an interesting can of worms – one that, as we'll see, echoes in discussions over numerous other vampire movies and TV serials covered in these pages, where the presence of more than one fanged lead has split audience affections. On the surface, in the case of *True Blood*, there should be no contest as to who qualifies as the show's pre-eminent pin-up. For one thing, for many fans, *True Blood*'s silver-tongued Southerner, Bill, is the most eligible bloodsucker to hit TV screens this century, no competition. (Proof, if such be needed, came when it was announced in 2009 that Stephen Moyer was engaged to the show's female lead, Anna Paquin – going some way to explain why their on-screen action was so hot.) For another, as *True Blood*'s uncontested hero, Bill's seldom far from the action, while the sinister Scandinavian Eric enjoys precious little screen time in the first series, and at time of writing, the second series has yet to be widely screened outside

Swedish actor Alexander Skarsgård as the ice-cool Nordic vampire, Eric Northman.

The fateful scene in True Blood *which entwines the fates of Eric, Sookie and Bill.*

the US. By way of example, in the '50 Greatest Vampires' poll run by UK magazine *SFX* – conducted before *True Blood* had seen much British exposure at all – Bill claims twenty-seventh place, presumably boosted by overseas votes and pure anticipation, while Eric languishes at number 45. However, stateside, where a *True Blood* cult had already evolved following the first season, Alexander Skarsgård described himself as 'shocked' by how quickly his character has become a fan favourite. 'I'm pretty much a glorified extra in season one. I didn't do much. I didn't expect anything, and I was overwhelmed when it started airing and I got all the reactions. It was very flattering, of course.'

Perhaps most importantly, the (aptly named) Nordic Northman is in striking contrast to the steamy atmosphere of the Deep South that characterises the show. From *True Blood's* opening credits, the inimitable spirit of bayou-bound Louisiana permeates the screen like a poisonously seductive miasma. A montage of images – of decay and desire, prejudice and passion – evokes the seedy underbelly of a region that remains, in many respects, America's heart of darkness. Kids in Ku Klux Klan robes and striking snakes flash across the screen, juxtaposed with sultry temptresses and rotting possums to

Right: 'Sookeh is Mahn!' At 170 years of age, Bill has a somewhat old-fashioned approach to relationships.

suggest a show that turns up the heat, leading the viewer into a dark and dangerous adult playground. *True Blood* is set in the small Louisiana town of Bon Temps – meaning 'good times' in the French spoken by many of the Creole natives, though these are good times likely to lead to some pretty bad places.

'I love the accent, I think it's a beautiful accent, it's really fun to do,' says Stephen Moyer (actually an Englishman from Essex) on preparing to play Bill, and the way in which the climate affects the steamy, languorous atmosphere of *True Blood*. 'It's one of those things where, when we went to Louisiana last year, I went, "Oh God, yeah, this is it. This is the South." As soon as you get there and see everybody just moving really slowly, once you are around that pace, and you see the South for what it's for. With the heat, you sort of understand why people move so slowly. You see why there is no extraneous movement.' Haunted by the ghosts of slavery and legends of voodoo, spiced by fiery Cajun cuisine and forgotten days of New Orleans as the USA's pre-eminent sin city, laidback Louisiana is as much a character in *True Blood* as any of its human – or, indeed, vampire – protagonists. Gothic authoresses Anne Rice and Poppy Z. Brite did much to suggest the Creole State as America's answer to mythic Transylvania with such novels as *Interview with the Vampire* and *Lost Souls*, but *True Blood* has confirmed that status in spades.

The character of Bill Compton both embodies and contrasts with *True Blood*'s Deep South decadence beautifully. He is almost literally a ghost of America's guilty past made flesh, a soldier who fought for the slave-owning South during the Civil War before an encounter with a vampire cut short both his military career and his mortal existence. While there's little ambivalence about the evils of slavery, the immoral plantation system built on its back does yield a certain guilty, amoral nostalgia – chiefly because ante-bellum Southern high society was the closest the US ever came to a European-style aristocracy (the bloodline of the classic bloodsucker). Like the nobility of the Old World, America's Southern high society had their own etiquette and culture, of elaborate balls and mint julep cocktails on the veranda, enjoyed by proud Southern gentlemen and elegant belles… in an era that still resonates with an overripe air of decadent opulence, soured by the taint of cruelty and racism simmering just beneath the surface.

While Bill Compton was a humble first lieutenant in the 48th Louisiana Infantry during his mortal life, rather than the colonel of popular cliché, he is most certainly a Southern gentleman. (Lieutenant Compton wasn't the only bloodsucker to enlist with the Confederacy in the Civil War – Jasper Hale rose through the ranks in Stephenie Meyer's *Twilight Saga*, while Jesse Hooker, vampire pack leader in *Near Dark*, still seems to be fighting the war in his own ruthless fashion.) Bill struggles with his dark side, and doesn't always win, but good manners and honour remain lodestones for the character. His very existence as a vampire stems from his strong moral code, which led a vampire – posing as a confederate widow – to convert rather than kill Bill back in 1865. 'I think that women in the modern world are attracted to the courtly manners of the nineteenth century, a time where men from the upper classes charmed women, but at the same time, men had to be men,' observes Moyer. 'This combination of being treated with respect by the man who can overpower you physically, that's very sexy.'

Eric locks horns with Bill Compton, played by Stephen Moyer.

'If you're their poster boy, the mainstreaming movement is in very deep trouble.'

Stephen Moyer's portrayal of Bill has true depth. He's a vampire trying to fit in with humanity – 'mainstreaming' in *True Blood* terminology – to do the right thing, but who can never escape what he is. 'What I love about Bill is that it's no accident our hero kills as many people in the first season as the murderer,' says the actor. 'He's a killer. He can't help himself. And I like the fact he's historical. As a confederate soldier, he doesn't like working on a computer and he keeps harking back to that period. He's also a man who has lost everything; from a war to his family to his mortality, and so he has pathos; his melancholy and yearning are attractive to play. Bill becomes a moral barometer for the show. The drug and sex addicts are human…' which is a vital point. While other screen vampires have excused their bloodlust by comparing their behaviour to human immorality, *True Blood* actually gives dramatic examples, with bad behaviour aplenty from the mortal characters to contrast with Bill's lapses from the path of righteousness.

This, perhaps, is the point where Eric Northman fits in. In contrast with Bill's Southern gentleman, Eric spends much of the first series doing a plausible impression of a Norse god, presiding over the human vampire groupies and his undead underlings at the Fangtasia bar. He has no interest in mainstreaming, appearing more than comfortable

Above: All the better to eat you with: Southern gentleman Bill Compton vamps out.
Below: Fangtastic in Fangtasia: Pam (Kristin Bauer), Eric and Chow (Patrick Gallagher)
prepare to partake of Bon Temps' local delicacies.

As the series progresses, Eric's interest in Sookie and her telepathic abilities becomes more personal than professional.

in his role as an undead predator, albeit one adapted to the new order where vampires live openly, if uneasily, among mortals. An original Viking, Northman's seniority – and commensurate power – make him the senior vampire in the district, officially known as 'Sheriff' within the hierarchy, and hence Bill's effective boss. 'Compared to Bill, I think Eric is so old,' says Alexander Skarsgård, who plays Eric. 'He's been around for a thousand years, so he kind of sees Bill as this naïve little kid. He's not even 200 years old. I think he sees him as kind of pathetic sometimes. In a way, Eric's jaded, because he's been around for a long time. It's hard to impress a guy like him, and it's hard to intrigue a guy like him.'

Somebody who does intrigue him is the spirited, telepathic waitress Sookie Stackhouse, the series' heroine played by Anna Paquin. The fact that Sookie and Bill are embroiled in a passionate cross-species affair creates dry tinder for future sparks to fly. Alexander explains that 'in the beginning, he used her and her ability to read minds. But as the story will progress, his interest becomes more personal and, of course, it creates drama and conflict, because Bill is very territorial.' Bill is protective – not so much a vampire with a conscience, as one who clings to his sense of honour as a remnant of his human identity. He rediscovers another aspect of that humanity in his love for Sookie, making for a potently romantic figure, the dangerous stranger who turns out to be a passionate knight in shining armour. By way of contrast, Eric Northman is the magnetic, arrogant anti-hero who lacks Bill's endearing vulnerability. 'I decided Bill's boss would be Bill's opposite in most ways,' says Charlaine Harris, the authoress whose novels inspired the series. 'Blonde, tall, imperious and in some ways surprisingly liberated, Eric almost leaped into the story.'

'He's very straightforward,' Alexander says of his character. 'He knows what he wants and he knows how to get it.'

'Humans ... honestly, Bill. I don't know what you see in them.'

In the same way, Eric leapt unexpectedly into the affections of many *True Blood* viewers, evidently responding to the character's naked power and icy confidence. 'He doesn't play any games,' observes Alexander of his character. 'He's very straightforward. He knows what he wants and he knows how to get it, basically. So, I just try to have fun with that directness to him. He's very grounded and very confident, and he knows what he wants, all the time, and he doesn't waste his time. Falling in love with humans and all that kind of stuff – some of the other vampires do that – is just a waste of time to him.' That cold unattainability just makes him more alluring somehow. Eric is untroubled by conscience, a calculating vampire undiluted by the desire to fit in – or mainstream – that characterises Bill. He is, in short, *True Blood*'s suave bad boy, the bloodsucker you couldn't take home to mother (or indeed grandmother in Sookie's case). Though not, Alexander Skarsgård insists, without his redeeming features.

'Season one was an introduction to Eric,' the actor told the Sci-Fi Wire website. 'You didn't see much more than the one side, which is him being the bad-ass vampire leader. In season two we go deeper, and you'll understand that he is more complex than that and has a sensitive side and a very loyal side. He can be a great friend. He doesn't like a lot of people, but if he likes you, then he's extremely loyal. For an actor, it's something I love to do, to go deeper and play more. I felt that after season one, people were always like, "Eric is the evil vampire," and I always defended Eric, because I don't see him as evil at all.' Skarsgård approaches each performance in *True Blood* with the same careful characterisation – a trademark that remains key to the power and appeal of the series, as well as the passionate response it inspires in viewers. Such passions stretch to those romantics who have fallen for the old-world charms of Bill Compton, or televisual 'fang bangers' who've been tempted by the ruthless, arcane power of Eric Northman. In the steamy, sinful world of *True Blood*, anything goes…

For seasoned vampire-watchers, the conflicting camps of Bill devotees and Eric groupies might seem oddly familiar. As we'll see in the following pages, similar scenarios have occurred over the years. In the popular TV show *Buffy the Vampire Slayer*, the title character's love interest surfaced in the competing vampiric forms of the virtuous Angel and the villainous Spike (even if he ultimately reforms). In *Interview with the Vampire*, audiences were offered the decent Louis in contrast to the decadent Lestat. Even in *Twilight*, the dreamy Edward meets competition in the feral form of James. In each case, the more sympathetic vampire is ebon-haired, his disreputable counterpart a blonde. And with spooky regularity, regardless of the intentions of authors, directors or scriptwriters, the fair-haired vampire has a tendency to steal both the show and the hearts of audiences from any more moral screen bloodsucker. The one obvious exception is *Twilight*, in which James doesn't survive long enough to pose any palpable challenge to the heartthrob status of Robert Pattinson's wan Edward.

What to make of this is another matter… that blondes have more fun? Maybe. Though assuming, for the sake of argument, that the vamps' hair colouring is incidental, then we're getting into the same territory that's puzzled countless problem columnists and behavioural psychologists. Why is it that some women keep falling for the wrong kind of man or, indeed, the wrong kind of vampire? Without going too deeply into such treacherous territory, there's some truth to the old adage that women love bastards – and you don't get much more evil than a ravenous vampire. It's a forbidden fantasy explored safely on the screen. Part of the appeal is the idea of reforming the bad boy, that love can heal troubled souls. That's certainly a significant part of the appeal of the romance between Sookie and Bill. Sometimes, though, a tamed rogue can paradoxically lose his appeal, and the lady still yearns for the dangerous thrill of unapologetic wickedness. Perhaps that's why some *True Blood* fans still find themselves smitten by the slick, deadly charisma of Eric – 'super-aggressive, ruthless and a killer' in Alexander's own words – lethal charms that may just prove irresistible, even for Sookie Stackhouse…

The Vampire Diaries

Ian Somerhalder as Damon Salvatore in
The Vampire Diaries

'Love sucks'

Mystic Falls, Virginia, is a sleepy Southern town – a close-knit community which happens to have a colourful Civil War history. But that's of small comfort to one of the town's teenagers, the beautiful Elena (Nina Dobrev). After losing both her parents in a car accident, Elena just can't engage with the world. She may be popular, but it's a struggle to carry on. That is, until new boy Stefan Salvatore (Paul Wesley) enrols at her school. Their paths soon cross; he's mature, charming and inexplicably fascinated by Elena. But his attentions quickly place her in danger, because Stefan is a vampire, an undead member of one of the town's founding families now come back to Mystic Falls after many years – and, although he doesn't drink human blood, he is soon joined by someone else with less self-control…

You might be forgiven for thinking that this all sounds a little familiar somehow. There are notable areas of overlap with Stephenie Meyer's hit novel, *Twilight*. Grown from a series of best-selling books into a film phenomenon, this blockbusting *Saga* can't help but cast a shadow over all subsequent screen interpretations of the fraught romance between mortal damsel and dashing bloodsucker. Actor Paul Wesley, though, was careful not to let Meyer's hero Edward Cullen colour his performance as Stefan. 'I specifically went out of my way not to watch *Twilight*,' he explains. 'I didn't want it to influence me in any way, because I knew that it was similar subject matter.' To be fair, the original *Vampire Diaries* book series, written by Lisa J. Smith, pre-dates *Twilight* by around fifteen years, but the latter's runaway success – together with popular series like *Buffy the Vampire Slayer* and *True Blood* – must surely have paved the way for this new TV sensation. Indeed, the screen Stefan is physically similar to Edward, with the same angular features and good-guy charisma.

So what is it that separates *The Vampire Diaries* from the *Twilight* juggernaut? 'The premise is the same – girl meets vampire – but once we're past that it does diverge,' assures executive producer Kevin Williamson, who was initially unsure about working on the series because 'I felt that it had been done and that nobody was going to do another vampire story. Then I began to realise that it was a story about a small town, about that town's underbelly and about what lurks under the surface.' So, although *The Vampire Diaries* borrows elements of other screen safaris into the realms of the undead – the Deep Southern setting, à la *True Blood*; *Buffy*'s blend of teen drama with a supernatural twist and, as in both of these, a tortured vampire struggling not to kill the human love he craves – the show still provides fresh thematic blood. And it's mostly thanks to Williamson's use of two vampiric leads. Entangled in the town's long and chequered history, the Salvatore brothers provide scope for *The Vampire Diaries* to be more than just another paranormal romance.

Which brings us to Stefan's older brother, Damon. Whereas moral Stefan prides himself on his self-control, his brother has no compunction at all in satisfying his baser appetites. 'He has such a good time doing it,' explains Ian Somerhalder, the actor who plays Damon. 'From his perspective, it's normal to eat people.' 'Stefan hates being a vampire … he just wants to experience life as a normal human being, whereas his brother is completely basking in this,' adds Wesley. 'He loves vampirism. He's enjoying it. He's more gluttonous, in that regard.' Damon arrives in Mystic Falls in pursuit of Stefan and, in contrast to his well-behaved brother, immediately sets about acquainting himself with the local cuisine. If he happens to take a liking to a young woman but doesn't kill her outright, he keeps her as a casual girlfriend, using his hypnotic influence to make her behave exactly as he wishes. Yet, with Damon beginning to tire of his role as lady-killer, it becomes apparent that he's more than just a foil to his brother's humane behaviour. Delectably devilish as the snake-eyed Salvatore may be, he's a character with an intriguing history behind him.

It's Founder's Day. I'm here to eat cotton candy and steal your girl.

'Whatever happened in the past, something happened between these two to yield an enormous amount of animosity, equally shared,' adds Somerhalder. 'Damon harbours a lot of anger toward Stefan for something he did in the past. He's angry. He feels like he's been wronged, very badly and he wants vengeance and redemption.' As Damon himself explains to his brother, 'I promised you an eternity of misery, so I'm just keeping my word.' Slowly, through stylish flashbacks to when the brothers became vampires in the 1860s, the audience can begin to piece together the great sadness which motivates Damon's cruelty. 'The whole idea is that Damon has lost all humanity, but we will see different sides of him, as the season starts to play out,' promises Somerhalder.

The use of brothers as the chief protagonists in *The Vampire Diaries* is an inspired choice: it's far more usual for vampire characters to belong to artificial 'covens' separated from their birth families by force (according to the requirements of the new group they've joined), or by choice (with newly turned vampires in search of companionship and a sense of belonging). As we shall see, the modern vampire myth has become all about surrogate families, with new unholy family units replacing natural blood relatives. One of the central plots in *Interview with the Vampire* concerns Lestat's attempt to create a deviant family with Louis and Claudia. The biker gang of *The Lost Boys* becomes a surrogate family for the character of Michael (Jason Patric), who finds himself alienated from his mother and brother; in *The Hunger*, Catherine Deneuve's character Miriam

Stefan (Paul Wesley) struggles to protect his fragile human love, Elena (Nina Dobrev).

forcibly recruits companions, at first irrespective of their feelings or their existing families. Seasoned aficionados might recognise the ambivalent relationship between two vampiric brothers from a lesser-known series of horror films, however. Low-budget flick *Subspecies* features a similar power struggle. Together with his sadistic vampire sibling Radu, the more moral, part-human Stefan plays out a complicated relationship, placing every mortal woman in the region under threat.

Stefan and Damon Salvatore share the same filial bond, pushed to breaking point by the circumstances in which they became vampires and, again, complicated by romantic entanglements. In a twist which would make Edward Cullen blush (if he only had a pulse), it seems that both brothers were, back in the 1860s, involved in a ménage-à-trois with a beautiful vampiress named Katherine (also played by Nina Dobrev). Teasing, morally ambivalent and definitely voracious, Katherine was unwilling to choose between her two beaus and elected to give them both the gift of eternal life, thus initiating a complicated rivalry which spans the centuries, inspiring Damon to follow Stefan back to Mystic Falls. Still, family is family…

'Make no mistake about it, Damon loves his brother,' insists Somerhalder. 'He's the only one he has. And to be honest with you, Stefan is the only person who truly understands Damon, who understands what he's been through, understands what he's coming from.' The fact that Elena is a dead ringer for Katherine adds a new dimension to the relationship between Stefan and Damon, since adoration for his maker, Katherine, is the only true weakness in Damon's otherwise perversely strong character. 'What I responded to is that every character in this book is dealing with loss,' says Williamson of the original stories behind the screenplay. 'They're dealing with death, they're dealing with life. There are

some big issues for some really young characters and that's what I tried to do with *Dawson's Creek* [Williamson's smash-hit nineties teen drama].'

Whilst Williamson is at pains to stress that *The Vampire Diaries* lacks *Dawson's Creek's* 'heightened psychobabble', it does share the ironic sense of humour of that popular earlier show and it is usually Damon who voices that humour. In contrast to Ian Somerhalder's previous role as the pretty but vacant Boone Carlyle in hit series *Lost*, Damon Salvatore is smart and humorous as he is carnal and devious. In opposition to Stefan's anguished soul-searching, Damon is entirely comfortable with his status as the black sheep. 'We, as humans, are drawn to someone, even if he is a complete bastard, because he has fun doing what he's doing,' opines Somerhalder. And if, as the actor asserts, 'The girls like the bad boy', then there is plenty to approve of in Damon's dark finesse. He's a consummate bad influence, frequently baiting his little brother about his self-imposed abstention from immoral indulgences such as supping human blood.

Left and above: 'Till death do us part. Like it or not, the Salvatore brothers seem bound for an eternity of sibling rivalry.

'Have I entered an alternate universe where Stefan is fun?'

Like the proverbial devil on one's shoulder, Damon encourages the satisfaction of those forbidden pleasures, and whenever Stefan's agonising over a moral dilemma, Damon is at hand to smile wryly at his little brother's continued pretensions to humanity. In keeping with the now-almost conventional uniform of the bad boy, Damon chooses to attire himself in black leather – albeit in a somewhat 'rock-lite' style – looking a lot like a young Rob Lowe, he is a million miles away from his brother's contented conventionality. To add insult to injury, when Damon is able to goad his virtuous brother into physical conflict, he's much faster and stronger than Stefan. It seems that Somerhalder's modern vampire mantra of 'sex, power and bravado' is 'alive' and well in his character. And even if the executive producer is averse to making a comparison with *Twilight*, Damon isn't afraid to say that Edward Cullen is – to quote an episode where Damon is seen sprawled nonchalantly on the bed reading Stephenie Meyer – 'so whipped'. It seems there is a new, complex and delightfully nasty vampire in town…

Being Human

Aidan Turner as Mitchell in *Being Human*

'They're amongst us.'

Meet Mitchell, hero of the cult BBC series *Being Human*, first broadcast in 2008. Mitchell's a regular guy in many respects… except that he happens to be a vampire, played by an actor widely reckoned to be the hottest thing to hit British screens in many a moon. The actor in question is Aidan Turner, whose easygoing Gaelic charm and dark, brooding good looks are enough to mesmerise viewers, even without the benefit of supernatural powers – as *Being Human*'s creator Toby Whithouse can attest, from his time viewing audition tapes when casting the vampire for his upcoming series. 'I got to Aidan and it was, "This is Mitchell,"' he recalls. 'My wife came from outside, and I said, "That's our Mitchell," and she was just staring at the screen. After a while I said, "You can go now. You can stop staring at the beautiful man."' 'With Aidan we all felt as soon as he walked into the room at the auditions that he was going to be a star,' concurs the show's producer Matthew Bouch. 'He looks great, has an incredible presence and an amazing charisma.'

'The pitch was: a group of friends buys a house, and it is about the stresses and strains it puts on their relationships,' recalls Toby Whithouse of *Being Human*'s rather unpromising beginnings. 'It was the dullest idea I'd ever heard. Completely independently, I had ideas for three characters: a guy named George, who was very punctilious, anal – a very old-fashioned romantic kind of guy; Annie, who's a little bit scatty, eccentric, lacking in confidence, borderline agoraphobic; and Mitchell, a recovering sex addict.' The concept clearly still lacked something, until Whithouse, half-joking, suggested that George might be a werewolf. To Toby's surprise, the producers liked the idea. From there, making Annie a spectre, desperate to unravel the circumstances of her own demise, and Mitchell a vampire, struggling to give up blood, were the next logical developments. The resultant script was something of an offbeat British crossbreed of *Friends* and *The Addams Family*, reinvented for the post-Anne Rice generation.

'Mitchell is 118 years old and to play someone like that is brilliant,' enthuses Aidan of the role he quickly made his own. 'With his maturity he has a certain kind of

Aidan Turner as the BBC's all-too-human vampire, Mitchell.

responsibility and a worldly experience that not all people have. He's not bothered by a lot of things – that side of him I aspire to be like. He's also like a father figure in some ways. I certainly think he's a father figure to Annie. He's the more mature person in the three-way relationship. Mitchell is the one where if something goes wrong, the others talk to him. I think he's just a cool guy.'

In many respects, however, Mitchell comes over more as an idealised older brother figure to many of the other characters in *Being Human*. He's capable and compassionate, with a shady past that gives him the extra allure of the reformed rebel – essential to any truly cool older brother. 'Everyone has a dark side that they don't expose too often – but when they do, you know about it,' observes Aidan – Mitchell is of course, after all, a vampire.

'I've got this friend. He says the human condition, human nature, being human, is to be cold and alone. Like someone lost in the woods.'

The BBC commissioned the first series of *Being Human* on the strength of a popular pilot, giving Toby Whithouse a critical opportunity to fine-tune the show. 'It was too Anne Rice,' he later observed of *Being Human*'s first incarnation. 'It was too lace and frills.' Toby recast a number of the characters, not least Mitchell, who'd been played by Guy Flanagan in the pilot as a gangly hipster, reminiscent of a Goth version of Jarvis Cocker, ex-singer with the chart-topping Brit-pop band Pulp. 'The way we've shifted the character from the pilot is to give him a little bit more comic material and make him less of an observer,' says Matthew of Aidan's reinterpretation of Mitchell. 'In the pilot we made him successfully feel like a vampire who was ageing and had seen a lot, but he didn't feel like he was part of that trio – and we wanted to get a sense of three friends who live together and get on. Aidan brings that sense of being an equal side of the triangle.' In the series, Mitchell becomes a more likeable vampire – tormented by bloodlust and the curse of immortality, perhaps, but also capable of being engaging, even disarmingly goofy.

'Mitchell is another in a long line of conflicted vampires (from the same lineage as Angel and Louis),' according to *SFX* magazine, 'but what sets him apart is a sense of optimism. While others mope, he smiles, ventures into the world and tries to make the best of things.' 'He wants to be more human and be a better person,' says Aidan. 'He wants to deal with it and face the sun.' This self-effacing humanity is perhaps what sets Mitchell apart from the legions of brooding, bestubbled bloodsuckers who've darkened our screens in recent years. While Mitchell does wear shades due to a slight photosensitivity, the midnight-black eveningwear favoured by more traditional vampires is out, in favour of shabby chic and fingerless gloves. Affable, softly-spoken, easygoing – with a keen sense of comic timing – Aidan's laidback performance makes it all the more shocking when Mitchell's darker side does take hold. 'It's a credit to Toby Whithouse as a writer to write a character, a vampire that's not [just] cloaks and fangs and blood and darkness and all the things that make a vampire what they are, but there's also other things, more important things, and I think he's really nailed it on the head. I think just playing a real guy's the best part of it,' says Aidan.

Mitchell enjoys some boy time with unlikely werewolf George (played by Russell Tovey).

Mitchell is a vampire who doesn't look out of place doing the washing up, or inviting the neighbours around for a cup of tea. His struggle to fight his addiction to blood, to turn his back on his previous life as a hero among his fellow vampires – to become not just human, but ordinary – is ironically what gives Mitchell his nobility. It's also the secret of Aidan's smouldering sex appeal for so many viewers. Vulnerability and plausibility are the traits that make him memorable – and so Mitchell feels less of a clichéd, unattainable fantasy figure than many higher profile bloodsuckers. He scored a respectable twenty-first place in *SFX*'s Top 50 Greatest Screen Vampires, while Stateside, in *Entertainment Weekly*'s Hottest New Vampire poll, readers voted Mitchell into the fifth spot – not quite up there with the big boys from *Twilight* and *True Blood*, but more than respectable for a vampire from such modest origins, a BBC series that's benefited from a tiny fraction of the budget and exposure of its lucrative American cousins.

Previous to playing the leading vamp in *Being Human*, Aidan had a brief role in *The Tudors*, the BBC's attempt to spark the interest of mainstream audiences in sixteenth-century history by adapting it as a steamy soap opera. Subsequent to setting pulses racing as Mitchell, Aidan was cast in the lead of *Desperate Romantics*, another attempt by the BBC to sell history – this time the world of Victorian art – by filming it through a heady filter of sex and suds. The series certainly had its critics, who felt *Desperate Romantics* featured rather too much soap – or even cheese – and not enough art or history, sacrificing accuracy in favour of tabloid-style storylines. But few could deny that Aidan Turner's performance, as the famous artist and notorious womaniser Dante Gabriel Rossetti, made the screen smoulder. There's certainly a superficial resemblance between *Being Human* and *Desperate Romantics*, in so much as both are genre hybrids. 'Being Human has elements of comedy, horror, soap and supernatural,' says Matthew Bouch. 'But what makes it a rich mix also makes it potentially quite tricky, as you don't want to allow

Mitchell's lair, in glaring contrast to the clichéd crumbling castles of classic Gothic.

any one of those elements to dominate too much. I think, with a combination of Toby's script and the brilliant cast, we've pulled it off.'

'You can piss your whole life away trying out who you might be. It's when you've worked out who you are that you can really start to live.'

While *Desperate Romantics* depicts the wild lives and loves of Victorian England's most scandalous group of celebrated young artists, *Being Human* takes the rather less glamorous setting of a house share in modern Bristol. It is *Being Human*'s low-key, kitchen-sink drama that gives the show much of its appeal, just as it's the key to Mitchell's self-deprecating charm. Despite the superficial similarities between Mitchell and Rossetti (the womanising artist Aidan plays in *Desperate Romantics*), in many respects, the roles could not be more different. 'What you want to do with every character you do, at least initially, is to make them likeable, and sometimes it's difficult, because he makes some crazy decisions,' observes Aidan of Rossetti. 'He looks after himself,' adds the actor, commenting on Rossetti's tendency to look after number one. 'He's a libertine, he's not incredibly moral and he's a chancer and a risk-taker, and he's talented, if not as talented as the rest of the painters, but talented nonetheless. He's a womaniser, he's passionate – he's a very passionate person about everything.' Mitchell shares Rossetti's passion, but in the vampire's case it's paired with a conscience – a more appealing combination in many respects.

As an intriguing aside, there is a connection between Dante Gabriel Rossetti and vampires, courtesy of an event depicted in the final episode of the first series of *Desperate Romantics* (though, typically, the show takes some liberties with the facts). In 1852, Rossetti's stunning wife Lizzie Siddal – who also modelled for many of his greatest paintings – died of a laudanum overdose, quite possibly a suicide. Overcome with grief, and perhaps guilt – he had been far from faithful during their marriage – Rossetti cast a journal containing all of his early poems into her coffin as a grand romantic gesture. It's a decision he lived to regret. In fact, this was the only copy of his early verse and seventeen years later the cynical Rossetti had his dead wife disinterred, in a desperate attempt to retrieve the journal. Reported glimpses of Lizzie's perfectly preserved corpse are said to have inspired the chilling scene in Bram Stoker's novel, *Dracula*, where Lucy Westenra's body is disinterred, and discovered to be similarly unaffected by the ravages of time – damning evidence that Lucy has become undead.

Unlike Rossetti, who displays no inclination to give up his womanising ways in *Desperate Romantics*, Mitchell struggles to turn his back on his own predatory heritage… not always successfully. He seduces a cute young nurse with inevitable results, and wracked with guilt, isn't there for her when she rises from the tomb as a vampire. The show's evil vampires use the newly-risen young nurse in their scheme to lure Mitchell back to the dark side, testing his resolve to breaking point. It's a subplot that not only highlights Mitchell's inner struggle, but also provides some of the steamiest scenes in the series, replete with enough plasma to remind viewers that *Being Human* is more than just a regular sitcom or soap. 'I have a pretty gory sex scene with a vampire called Lauren,' recalls Aidan with a guilty grin. 'She's really hot and we're covered with blood and we're having sex in the bathroom. That's pretty disgusting. It wasn't for us – we were loving it! Everyone was really sick. I remember finishing the scene and walking out and someone said it was absolutely disgusting, but I thought it was really sexy!' Didn't Aidan have any reservations about playing such bloodthirsty scenes? 'No, that's the fun part!' he laughs.

Van Helsing

Richard Roxburgh as Count Vladislaus Dracula in *Van Helsing*

'How does it feel to be a puppet on my string?'

From the towering heights of his imposing Gothic stronghold, Count Vladislaus Dracula is lord of all he surveys – a sardonic, supernatural monarch with a wry commanding stare and a mercurial sense of Romany style. Yet while the Prince of Darkness traditionally dominates any film he appears in – just as Vladislaus effortlessly rules his own twilit domain – in 2004's *Van Helsing*, as its title makes plain, the spotlight was on his mortal foe. This time, Dracula's nemesis wasn't to be some fussy grey-haired professor or a grim, crucifix-brandishing medical man, but a dashing young swashbuckler of the old school. The casting of Australian heartthrob Hugh Jackman in the title role made doubly sure that, for once, most eyes would be on the vampire-hunter, not the Count…

The performer they chose to don the cloak for this action-packed duel between good and evil was another Australian actor named Richard Roxburgh. Roxburgh first captured Hollywood's attention playing the villain in a very different sort of picture. In the hit 2001 musical *Moulin Rouge* he played the depraved Duke of Monroth, an aristocratic English cad in the classic mould, a wealthy moustachioed bounder willing to sink to any depths to have his wicked way with the heroine. Richard could perhaps have brought something similar to his interpretation of Dracula – there have certainly been some eminent English Draculas over the years. But, while he retains some of the Duke's aristocratic arrogance, Roxburgh's Count is very much a creature of wild, Eastern European elegance, a product of Transylvania's untamed landscape of impenetrable forests and dizzying ravines, presided over by ancient, lofty castles. And so, *Van Helsing* introduced a bold new breed of Dracula, an amalgam of the austere overlord of yesteryear and someone a little more suave and dashing.

'There is obviously darker hair and I wanted a sense of a Romany king or leader, a faded aristocrat,' the blonde actor said of taking on the mantle of cinema's best-known bloodsucker. 'I liked that gypsy element. So the character looks nothing like me… I didn't want the wardrobe to be too visible. We had these amazing Italian women who did a terrific job of creating the look of a faded aristocrat. The look is not flowingly romantic though a couple of people did mention the name Adam Ant at times.' (Adam, vocalist with Adam and the Ants, helped popularise the piratical, dandy highwayman look among New Romantic club kids in the '80s.) Certainly, though Richard Roxburgh's Count does wear a lot of black, his look is less sombrely funereal than many of his predecessors. With an earring, discreet ponytail and selection of ornate outfits for formal occasions, this Dracula brings a little Bohemian chic to the party, with the air of a sardonic playboy, too well-heeled and well-bred to concern himself with convention. 'I prefer to think of him as a muscular Dracula with a lot of rage, who I think got a raw deal,' said Roxburgh. 'He made a pact with the Devil to live forever, but now can't feel anything. He's still a gentleman, just a gentleman who made some dark decisions.'

The script details a few of those 'dark decisions', as Dracula hints at the unholy circumstances which transformed him from a medieval Transylvanian prince to a creature of the night. He introduces himself as 'Count Vladislaus Dragulia. Born 1422. Murdered 1462.' Vlad the Impaler, the real-life Wallachian warlord who inspired Stoker's original novel *Dracula*, did actually sometimes sign himself 'Vladislaus', though he actually lived between 1431 and 1476. The Count's background is reminiscent of that given to Gary Oldman in *Bram Stoker's Dracula* twelve years before, which was one of the first films to make explicit the link between the vampire Count, and the real-life fifteenth-century Romanian tyrant. Early drafts of the script reportedly envisaged *Van Helsing* as a follow-up to the Oldman *Dracula*, though such plans were shelved early on in favour of a wholly fresh, more light-hearted and lively approach. According to *Van Helsing*'s script, after he was mysteriously murdered, Dracula made a pact with the Devil, granting him immortality and supernatural powers, but at a terrible price. The story establishes connections between the Count, his nemesis Van Helsing (who Dracula reveals is also an immortal, who murdered him in 1462), and the film's heroine, Anna Valerious (last of her line, both kin to and ancient rivals of Dracula). The vampire-hunting Anna is, incidentally, played by Kate Beckinsale, fresh from her role as undead assassin Selene in *Underworld* the previous year.

'I have no heart, I feel no love. Nor fear, nor joy, nor sorrow. I am hollow... and I will live forever.'

Of course, every actor who comes to the role of the immortal Count lives under the shadow of preceding performances, and this was doubly so in *Van Helsing*, which sought to strike a balance between ringing the changes and paying due reverence to tradition. It was produced by Universal, a studio famous for their classic monster movies of the 1930s and '40s, and director Stephen Sommers conceived of *Van Helsing* as an action adventure that pays tribute to the same seminal films that gave us instantly iconic versions of Hollywood's greatest monsters. It was Universal who first dressed Dracula in an opera cape and styled him with slicked-back black hair; Universal who first put bolts through the neck of Frankenstein's monster, surmounted with the trademark square-topped skull. 'The movie opens in black and white,' Sommers explained of *Van Helsing*'s prologue. 'It

Dracula's glamorous brides attracted nearly as much attention as the Count himself.

fits because the opening sequence is sort of the climax of the original *Frankenstein* movie condensed into seven minutes. The opening line in my movie is, "It's alive! It's alive! It's alive!" It's paying honour to the original. For the people who know, remember and love the original monster movies, I'm going to blow their socks off.'

Van Helsing enjoyed a budget that dwarfed those of Universal's black-and-white originals, (during the lean years of the Great Depression, the studio made these monster movies to stave off bankruptcy), allowing for more impressive crowd scenes. One side effect of this is to change the very nature of Count Dracula's persona. In many versions of the Dracula story, a profound undertone of the Count's private tragedy is loneliness. Typically, he lives all but alone in his Transylvanian sanctuary; a once proud lord, now reduced to residing in a dust-choked ruin manned by a skeleton staff – a monosyllabic butler perhaps, and sometimes a trio of bestial Brides, more like troublesome pets than true soulmates. In *Van Helsing*, things are very different. The Count hosts grand costume balls as befits a true Transylvanian aristocrat, and commands a legion of adoring followers and loyal minions. If Richard Roxburgh's character is driven by inner torment, it is not born of loneliness.

In *Van Helsing*, Sommers pits his titular hero against a menagerie of classic monsters, peopling his lavishly Gothic sets – crumbling medieval stonework lit by elaborate candelabras – with updated versions of horror icons of the black-and-white era, resurrecting not just Frankenstein's monster, but any number of werewolves. 'What really interested me was that Steve wasn't looking to run from Dracula's history, or indeed the horror genre in general,' said Richard Roxburgh of what first attracted him to the Sommers production. 'He used it as a springboard and took it somewhere else with all the technology now available. I loved the sequences that really drew from the flickering lamplight and huge shadows of 1930s horror, which, in some ways, I feel hasn't been

The Count romances Anna (played by Kate Beckinsale) in the lavish ballroom scene.

surpassed. But I also got to fly on wires, which was great. I love that stuff.' The generous budget allotted by Universal to *Van Helsing* shows in the spectacular set-pieces – explosive, high-flying battles against dizzying backdrops of Transylvanian grandeur. In contrast to the atmospheric chillers that inspired it, *Van Helsing* is very much an action picture, and its Count a highly physical, energetic Prince of Darkness, particularly compared to more stately early portrayals – most notably that of Hungarian actor Bela Lugosi in Universal's classic 1931 adaptation, *Dracula*.

Richard emphasises that he is a huge fan of Lugosi's Count, whom he describes as having 'real lustre and appeal', even for today's audiences. Most obviously, he borrows from Bela the actor's distinctive tones, which gifted clichéd Counts with a Hungarian accent ever since Lugosi's immortal performance. 'The trick was avoiding the *Sesame Street* Count,' said Roxburgh of his careful vocal characterisation for the part. In common with every other classic Universal monster, Bela's Dracula has become a victim of both the passage of time and his own success, since, in his case, familiarity has not led to contempt so much as affection. This is fine for any director looking to reinvent the Prince of Darkness as a puppet that teaches kids to count, but not such good news for those seeking to retain an edge of dignified menace for the vampire aristocrat. Richard Roxburgh combated this tendency towards camp by focusing on giving the familiar figure of Dracula some much-needed depth: 'I always felt that I wanted to anchor the character in the sense of an actual human being, a person who feels that frustration and is terribly tired of the situation that he finds himself in – three wonderful Brides notwithstanding.'

No, no, no. Do not fear me, everybody else fears me. Not my Brides.

The Count's Transylvanian Brides have been a feature in the story of Dracula since the original novel of 1897, though frequently relegated to the role of creepily erotic walk-on parts. *Van Helsing* sees this trio of vampiric vixens take centre stage – not least as the Count's able, bat-winged allies, demonic harpies that swoop from the sky in one of the film's most memorable battles, falling on their husband's foes like erotic birds of prey in a special-effects tour de force. Ugo.com even gives the seductive trio a collective place in their 'Top 50 Sexiest Vampires'. 'Unfortunately, the Brides meet a triad of grisly ends,' sighs the site, 'but leave us wondering: is Dracula a Mormon or something? Why does he get to have three Brides?' Silvia Colloca is well placed to give us a clue. She not only plays lead vampiress in *Van Helsing*, she's also a huge fan of vintage horror. A self-confessed 'monster freak', Silvia notes 'something […] really special about Dracula […] is the constant search for blood, which is enticing and sensual. And which is why the Count has three Brides.' As Silvia suggests, Dracula's bloodlust hints at the kind of virility only a trio of mates could satisfy.

In *Van Helsing* the Count's Transylvanian harem are not only given names, but also individual personalities and dialogue – a far cry from the usual scenario, where Dracula's Brides are required to do little more than pout and snarl seductively before being despatched with a handy stake. *Van Helsing*'s own ladies of the night are played by gorgeous actresses Silvia Colloca (as Verona), Josie Maran (Marishka) and Elena Anaya (Aleera), bedecked in exotic finery – like sultry Gothic gypsy princesses – that compliments the Eastern European style of their vampire lord. 'Verona has never smiled,' says Silvia of her role. 'She's very focused, she's very tempered. She's older and she's been there before, so they're no fun for her. It's not a laughing matter. She just needs to go into it. But Marishka, she's playing around, she's young and she thinks that she can toy with Van Helsing, and she doesn't really know what she's thinking. And they were laughing. Yes, she does enjoy fighting along with Aleera. But Verona is very concentrated and focused, and she's probably more inclined to lead the Brides in the attack. And she freaks out.'

It might be stretching matters beyond breaking point to suggest that *Van Helsing* gives the familiar *Dracula* saga a feminist spin. But Dracula's Brides not only provide the key to the plot, but also to one unique aspect of Richard Roxburgh's interpretation of the vampire Count. In many ways he seems eminently reasonable, if ruthless. 'Why can't they just leave us alone?' Dracula ponders of his human opponents at one point. 'We never kill more than our fill. And less than our share. Can they say the same?' In fact, the thing destined to upset this delicate balance is the desire of the Count's Transylvanian harem to have offspring. In other words, in *Van Helsing*, the Brides of Dracula become broody – and despite his declaration that he has no heart, the Count is only too eager to oblige. This is the Prince of Darkness as proud prospective dad – Dracula as a pushover to the demands of his beloved trio of beautiful Brides. 'I tried very hard to sexualise his relationship with his Brides,' reflected Richard Roxburgh of his interpretation of Dracula as an aloof gypsy aristocrat. 'They are stunning and one of them is my bride to be in real life. I'm marrying Silvia Colloca. We are marrying in September in Italy – so Stephen cast very well indeed!'

Underworld

Kate Beckinsale as Selene in *Underworld*

'An Immortal Battle for Supremacy.'

Few vampire films can have relied so strongly upon the sexual magnetism of their lead player as 2003's *Underworld*. But in this case, the focus of reviews, audience attention – and the director it appears – was very firmly on the film's star, Kate Beckinsale... and more specifically, it has to be said, on Kate's perfect, pert posterior, which the costume department had poured into a skin-tight catsuit, and which the cameras follow with much the same devotion as the eyes of Ms Beckinsale's legion of besotted fans.

Underworld is set at the climax of a six-century-old war between vampires and werewolves, known in the film as 'Lycans'. Beckinsale plays Selene, leader of an elite squad of undead assassins known as 'Death Dealers', gun-toting vampires tasked with eliminating their sworn shape-shifting foes. To accomplish her mission, the ice-cool Selene is equipped with an impressive array of automatic weaponry, silver throwing stars, and some formidable martial arts skills – topped off with *that* figure-hugging, shiny black catsuit.

The catsuit is entirely appropriate attire for Kate's character – one of many examples of the female of the vampire species as a thoroughly feline creature. Not only does she drop to the floor, ready for action, with appropriate agility, but Selene slinks through the film with a lofty feline insouciance. Though this is one pedigree sex kitten with sharp claws, turning in a performance *Entertainment Weekly* praise as 'pale, pouty, eerily still' in their '20 Greatest Vampires of All Time'. The catsuit has long been cinema's costume of choice for the elegantly physical femme fatale. In 1992 Michelle Pfeiffer raised a number of eyebrows – and even more temperatures – appearing in a similarly skin-tight ensemble as Catwoman in *Batman Returns* (a performance some credit for mainstreaming fetish wear in fashion). In vampire history, Carroll Borland wore one way back in 1935 for *Mark of the Vampire*, while the stunning, dark-eyed French vamp Musidora set the ball rolling in 1915's silent cinema serial, *Les Vampires*, as the cabaret singer Irma Vep. (The poisonously sultry Irma Vep may not have been a 'real' vampire, but her anagrammatic name is pretty incriminating.)

English rose Kate Beckinsale as the undead Death Dealer Selene.

Unlike such Gallic or American femme fatales, however, Kate Beckinsale's Selene drew on the actress's own English roots. The prototype of the classy English femme fatale, a pallid rose with deadly thorns, was surely set in *The Avengers*. A hip, somewhat surreal British spy series made in the swinging '60s, *The Avengers* is most warmly remembered for its heroines, who were more than a match for any man. Sassy and classy, these well-spoken spy queens – played by Honor Blackman, Diana Rigg and Linda Thorson – fought crime in figure-hugging bodysuits inspired by the kinky couture found in fetish clubs. It was daring stuff long before S&M style became a catwalk commonplace, and several episodes were banned in the US. For viewers of a certain age, Kate Beckinsale's Selene brought memories of *The Avengers* flooding back. 'Being exposed in one's youth to a leather-clad Diana Rigg in *The Avengers* had an effect on many males of my generation – and I fear I am no different,' confessed the *Daily Mail*'s film critic in his review of *Underworld*.

Essentially, the heroines of *The Avengers* share with Selene an unmistakable air of class, of the prim English lady with a cut-glass accent whose carefully cultivated demeanour conceals a hot-blooded spirit. In common with her cultured forebears in *The Avengers*, Kate's more than just a pretty face, having studied French and Russian literature at Oxford's exclusive New College. In 1993 she decided to abandon her degree to concentrate on her acting career, having already secured a part in Kenneth Branagh's big-screen version of the play *Much Ado About Nothing*. Still, her Oxford education and pedigree in Shakespearean drama have helped lend Kate the image of an innocent abroad in Hollywood, a chaste English ingénue in the world's capital of vulgarity. 'I've never been drunk even,' she confessed in an interview to promote *Underworld*. 'I've never taken drugs. I've never had a one-night stand. I haven't done anything that I'm really ashamed of. So, if somebody says, so, do you wear underwear? Well, no I don't.'

'Our war has waged for centuries, unseen by human eyes. But all that is about to change.'

The attitudinal, gun-toting babe has become a staple of action cinema. Dodging accusations of sexism as well as bullets, she's proven that she dies as hard as any of the boys, perhaps down to her image as an 'empowered' woman, though this is a point of some contention. In due course, it's fair to say, the ass-kicking action heroine has become something of a genre cliché. However, in their 'Top 50 Vampires' list, *SFX* insist that, 'Selene is more than just a cliché – she's the pinnacle of the form. While Milla Jovovich in *Ultraviolet* and Angelina Jolie in the *Lara Croft* films try to pull off the gal-with-guns, kick-ass angel shtick (with varying degrees of success), Kate Beckinsale nails it so effortlessly, you know that she's the yardstick by which all pretenders will be measured from here on in. The look is right. The attitude is right. The moves are right. The way she steps casually off rooftops, plunges hundreds of feet, then lands with the grace of a cat is right. The ass is so very, very right. No wonder that she's the top-rated female vampire in this list.' As this less than politically-correct assessment of Selene suggests, though, the action heroine flick isn't wholly bulletproof among feminists.

Double-barrelled action in Underworld.

As far as the actress herself is concerned, however, *Underworld* was a rare opportunity to play the boys at their own game. 'I thought it was great,' she said of her character Selene. 'I must say, I really do [and] seriously always have *loved* action movies. When you get sent a great script for an action movie, and want to play the boy's part... You know, because normally... it's like in *Die Hard*. I don't want to be sitting on an airplane making phone calls. I want to be blowing up the elevator shaft! And that doesn't happen very often. And when it does happen that the female is the lead of the film, and it's an American movie and it's a bit camp... and I've always wanted to do something like *La Femme Nikita*.' (Of course, if Kate had done her horror homework, she'd have known that Anne Parillaud, star of *La Femme Nikita*, reprised her role as a lethal assassin in *Innocent Blood*, the 1992 vampire flick.

One criticism of the trilogy is that it drifts too far from its Gothic roots, to the point where the fact that the protagonists are vampires and werewolves seems almost incidental. 'I wasn't in a big rush to read it because I had a feeling it was going to be a B-movie, kind of schlocky horror thing when I heard it was werewolves and vampires,' Kate revealed, on the subject of her first impressions of the script. 'And I didn't fancy running about in a white nightgown, screaming and all that. But it happened to be that the director had done all these drawings that he'd sort of put inside the script. So, I saw those and said, 'Oh! Okay, that looks kind of like what I'd like seeing.'

> 'Like the weapons of the previous century, we, too,
> would become obsolete. Pity, because I lived for it.'

'We heal like vampires do,' explained Kate of *Underworld*'s radical new breed of undead. 'We don't have a whole lot about garlic and crucifixes. We don't have any of that. It's much more high-tech than that. The werewolves kill with ultraviolet bullets that shoot

More of the extensive armoury of high-tech weaponry employed by Selene.

daylight into us. I can jump from this great height and land. We don't turn into bats. None of the stuff that kind of makes me feel a bit [creepy] about doing a vampire movie is really in it, which I was kind of glad about. We shoot the werewolves with silver-nitrate bullets. It's really just having a couple of big-ass Glocks.' 'Wait, she is a vampire in the movie?' quipped Hollywood.com, who placed her at number five of their 'Top 10 Sexiest Vampires'. 'Most people stop paying attention after the tight spandex outfits.'

Discussion of Kate Beckinsale's role – and predominantly, how good she looked in her kinky, skin-tight costume – has tended to eclipse other aspects of the film. The project began when director Len Wiseman and his friend Kevin Grevioux (who went on to play a werewolf in the film) decided they wanted to make a werewolf movie. Anxious to get away from the clichés of the genre, the two elected to write a script in which the werewolves were faced with an equally dangerous foe. And so, the idea of pitting them against vampires was born. The story evolved into a complex plot, which combined elements of action flicks and conspiracy thrillers to create an intricate world where power politics and frenetic gunplay explode over a dark canvas of slick contemporary Gothic. Perhaps the most controversial element was the idea of a forbidden romance between a vampire and a werewolf, which some were quick to compare with Shakespeare's classic tragedy, *Romeo and Juliet* – the story of two 'star-crossed lovers' torn apart by their feuding families.

'That was kind of a dangerous one,' Wiseman observed of *Underworld*'s romantic subplot. 'I'm kind of afraid of all that's corny. I do shy away from that stuff. So the minute [the studio] came up with this, "Why don't we do this kind of *Romeo and Juliet*?" [...] I thought it was the lamest idea I'd ever heard in my whole life. I'm already trying to go to studios and pitch that it's vampires versus werewolves. I always feel like that, to me, sounds like a B-movie. Just the nature of it being a werewolf [film], it's something you've got to get over when you're pitching. When the whole Romeo-and-Juliet thing came in to play, it was really just to set up the state of the two races. Instead of Montagues and Capulets, there are werewolves and vampires. [To create] that tension, the forbidden nature of them being together, that was much more the thrust of the romance than just the all-out love story.' In truth, the romance between Kate Beckinsale's Death Dealer and the werewolf/vampire hybrid played by Scott Speedman is not one of the film's highlights – there's little chemistry between the two, with Speedman suffering from a lack of charisma throughout. Nevertheless, the angle probably helped the director convince Sony to finance the picture.

The studio was taking something of a chance on Len Wiseman, as *Underworld* was to be his debut feature. And, though he did have an impressive number of credits as a director on commercials and music videos under his belt, this was hardly enough to impress hardcore horror fans, weary of soulless, heavily polished Hollywood product, riddled with computer-generated explosions and frantic editing, but devoid of plot or character. Many suspected that Wiseman's background would inevitably lead to an MTV-style exercise in style over substance. Yet the director insists he kept computer effects to a minimum, stating '[My] pitch for this was I wanted to go back to prosthetic creatures. I didn't want to do CG. I just think that nothing has really scared me since an *Aliens* or *American Werewolf* [*in London*].' He and his co-author Kevin Grevioux also found support from the British actor Bill Nighy, who they cast as the powerful vampire elder, Viktor.

Nighy insists that *Underworld* was far from a cynical, empty exercise. 'I was thrilled because I like vampires,' he said of being asked to play Viktor. 'I actually dig all this stuff. I'm a real enthusiast and I thought *Underworld* was as hip and as cool a script, a vampire/werewolf script, as you'll ever find anywhere in the world. And they're believers, you know? They're real enthusiasts. They didn't just make a vampire movie because they were trying to get into the movies or something and it was their first movie. They chose very carefully. It was the movie that they wanted to make and they wanted it to be their first movie. And it went straight in at number one in America and made a whole bunch of money, and they're really, really, really, really nice guys, so I was thrilled.'

In truth, perhaps there was actually a little too much content in *Underworld*. The involved plot and epic backstory provided plenty of chances for spin-offs and sequels, but equally left some bewildered viewers feeling as though they'd come in halfway through the saga. But too much content is a rare criticism to level at a big-budget Hollywood blockbuster. Bill Nighy's point that the level of depth the scriptwriters put into the story may have bemused casual audiences is fair enough, but it did demonstrate the filmmakers' own passionate commitment to the project. *Underworld* is not a great vampire film, but it is a master class in creating a big-screen sex symbol, in the unforgettable shape of Selene, surely one of cinema's most memorable femme fatales. As the *Times* put it, justifying Kate's place in their own list of top vamps: 'It's Selene's skin-tight leather catsuit that does the trick. It certainly got the attention of Len Wiseman, *Underworld* director and now Beckinsale's husband.'

Angel

David Boreanaz as Angelus in Angel

'Fight evil, bring Buffy home.'

It's a common fantasy – a mysterious guardian watching over you from the shadows. In the hit TV series, *Buffy the Vampire Slayer*, David Boreanaz played out precisely this dream in the role of Angel, the vampire with a soul who takes it upon himself to protect the show's heroine, Buffy Summers, from harm. The character debuted in the first episode of the series in 1997, initially as an enigmatic presence, dropping dark hints to warn Sunnydale's slayer of imminent danger. Angel was the very image of romantic cliché – tall, dark and handsome with a broad, brooding brow and sartorial style in spades... suggesting that his elusiveness concealed a sinister secret. ('Angel was sort of like a vamp Fonzie: effortlessly cool, with meticulously coiffed hair and a fondness for black leather,' according to *Entertainment Weekly*'s 2009 feature, '20 Greatest Vampires'.)

'Angel is a 242-year-old vampire with a conscience,' explains David. 'He was born in Ireland, he comes from a wealthy family; he was a bit of an aristocrat in his early years. He meets Buffy, and he falls in love. The common thread is that they both understand, Buffy is a vampire slayer and so she doesn't have a normal life, she's not like other kids in high school. She has powers that control her, to fight evil.' The course of a love affair between slayer and vampire – even one with a soul like Angel – is not destined to run smooth. 'She realises he's a vampire, she's freaked and he's freaked,' says David. 'They deal with it. They don't think of the consequences.' There were consequences for the show as well as the characters, and when their star-crossed romance threatened to dominate the story, *Buffy*'s producers decided it was time to bring the relationship to a suitably dramatic end at the climax of the third series.

However, by this point, both Angel and the actor David Boreanaz had become too popular to simply disappear back into the darkness. So in 1999, Joss Whedon – responsible for creating *Buffy* – gave the character his own series, *Angel*, in which TV's favourite conflicted vampire sets up a detective agency in LA, specialising in confronting the forces of evil. That show lasted five seasons, finally winding up in 2005

Over his six-year career as Angel, David has inevitably presided over many changes to the character. Not to mention Angel's colourful previous existence, as revealed in numerous dramatic flashbacks. As Angelus he was the most infamous vampire of his age, killing his own family ('my parents were great – tasted like chicken'), before embarking upon a sadistic reign of terror. It was cut short in 1898, when a gypsy curse reunited Angel with his soul, reigniting his dormant conscience and forcing the horrified vampire to confront the atrocities he'd perpetrated as Angelus.

'Being this character is very diverse,' observes David Boreanaz of Angel. 'There's different parts of him and personalities that I find in every show.' The story arcs have enabled the actor to develop Angel into a multi-faceted character. When we first meet him, Angel is, in David's own words, 'a man on a mission, so to speak, that is atoning for his sins and trying to make something of himself. A lot of people today look in the mirror and what do they see? Are they afraid to look in the mirror and see what's really there? That's a big question for Angel's character. It's something that… you know? I know I wake up and look in the mirror and try and see the truth.' That reflective, guilt-ridden persona remains part of Angel's character throughout, contributing a brooding sensitivity some fans find irresistible. 'I'm not afraid to cry,' says Boreanaz. 'Tears are a form of expression and that's sexy.'

> 'I'm weak. I've never been anything else.
> It's not the demon in me that needs killing Buffy, it's the man.'

As *Buffy the Vampire Slayer* progressed, the show's heroine too found it increasingly irresistible. Joss Whedon, creator of the series, has firm ideas about the moral values that lie behind his 'Buffyverse'. A recurring theme is redemption through suffering and sacrifice and few characters illustrate this better than Angel. *Buffy the Vampire Slayer* didn't just develop as a series; it palpably matured. It was natural for a show centred on high school, using adolescent life as a metaphor for wider issues, to grow with its main characters, attracting an ever-broadening audience in the process. While some teen TV shows are happy to pretend their leads are adolescents for as long as the ratings will support it, in *Buffy* the characters mature and ultimately graduate, moving the setting from Sunnydale High to the Sunnydale Campus of the University of California.

The graduation of Buffy and her fellow students forms the climax of the third series – the two-part 'Graduation Day' story also depicting the culmination of the romance between Buffy and Angel. The relationship had developed gradually over the preceding episodes, from the awkward flirtations of season one, to the building passion of the second series. It was in 'Surprise', the thirteenth episode of season two, that the crunch came and Angel and Buffy finally confessed their feelings for each other. 'They consummate their relationship,' explains David Boreanaz, 'and with that his soul is lifted and he becomes evil again, and he starts to go back to his old ways, because he's lost his conscience, and he's now Angelus.' In a typical Whedon-esque twist, the sting in the tail of the gypsy curse that gave Angel back his soul is that it will be taken away again should he ever find

Angel's career in Buffy *and* Angel *saw him tussling with a weird and wonderful range of monsters and villains.*

true happiness, and thus Buffy's true love transforms into her deadliest enemy, as Angelus reverts to type.

Meanwhile, some ghosts from Angel's dark past surface in Sunnydale in the shape of the vampires Spike and Drusilla, an anarchic undead couple destined to cause trouble for Buffy and her friends. They were also destined to become fan favourites – particularly Spike, who worms his way into the affections of both the *Buffy* audience and the slayer herself. Season two concludes with Buffy being forced to slay Angel, her true love – a ritual killing which both consigns him to hell and destroys her psychologically. He would return in the following series, having rediscovered his soul, but now painfully aware that yielding to his feelings for Buffy invites inevitable disaster. Their romance is a parable of forbidden love – in high-school terms, of a teenager with an older man, though it can be taken as a metaphor for any sexual attraction where yielding to temptation carries too high a price; be it an office affair or the betrayal of marriage vows. Angel leaves *Buffy the Vampire Slayer* with the chastening lesson that sometimes, true love is not enough, that sometimes the noble thing to do is to simply walk away.

Angel offered the opportunity for the character to explore new challenges and dilemmas in a series set in the more conventionally adult framework of a gritty detective show, albeit one with the supernatural spin familiar to the Buffyverse. According to Joss Whedon, 'We wanted a much darker show, darker in tone. It is set in Los Angeles because there are

Angel takes the lead.

a lot of demons in LA and a wealth of stories to be told. We also wanted to take the show a little older and have the characters deal with demons in a much different way. Buffy is always the underdog trying to save the world, but Angel is looking for redemption. It's those two things that creatively make the shows different.' During Angel Investigations' conflicts with the forces of darkness, the series addresses such issues as racism and the pressure to bow to corrupt authority. Angel even faces up to the responsibilities of being a father. 'With *Buffy*, it was kind of a rite of adolescence; like coming into the world and trying to define yourself,' explains Joss Whedon. 'With *Angel*, it's more about the choices you've already made and living with them and improving upon yourself at a time when most people have kind of become inflexible.'

'For a taciturn, shadowy guy, I've got a big mouth.'

However, just like *Buffy the Vampire Slayer*, the series was far from uniform in tone, with numerous flashes of humour to balance the darker aspects. 'We knew we had a great actor in David Boreanaz and a pretty good character that could stand on its own two legs and have his own show,' said David Greenwalt, co-creator of *Angel*. 'I think what we realised – sort of the frosting on the cake – was that David is a great comedian. David loves to make fun of himself and he loves it when we do crazy things with him.'

Buffy's beloved in contemplative mood.

While the scripts have provided plenty of romance for Angel, it's never destined to run smooth for the troubled vampire.

The humour of the character has been part of Angel's appeal since early on, with co-star Charisma Carpenter, who plays Cordelia, describing him as 'a total cornball meets Prince Charming'. Seeing the serious, brooding vampire sing out of tune or make a clumsy mistake, makes him, if not human, at least disarmingly funny. 'The best thing about [s]etting him up is seeing him miserably fail,' says the actor himself, 'because it is a dark-[s]ided character and his humour really comes [out] if he's being humiliated or if he's got [e]gg all over his face. Then you see his humiliation and you see that "fumbley-ness" that [h]e has, and that's humour.'

'It's always fun playing evil Angel or sarcastic, witty Angel,' adds David of the many [f]aces of his vampire with a conscience. 'It's hard to say which one I enjoy more than the [o]ther. I really enjoy all of them.' It's indicative of the character's enduring appeal and [l]ongevity that David Boreanaz has managed to create a convincing character with so [m]any facets. 'I never really played Angel as a vampire,' reflected the actor, during the [f]ilming of the fifth season of *Angel*. 'I played him as more of a person. I think that's been [m]y take on him, to play him with a sense of a guy who's really old and he's got a lot of [t]roubles, and he's holding down a big cross. So I never played into the vampirism, I just let the story unfold. I'm just playing a character and still developing him.' Sadly, to the surprise of those working on the series, the network pulled the plug on *Angel* at the end of its fifth season, making it David Boreanaz's swansong as the well-loved character.

Angel is far from the only undead detective to have pounded the beat on the small screen, and several other scriptwriters have attempted to crossbreed crime and horror, with plots oddly reminiscent of *Angel*. Ten years before *Angel* debuted, the network unleashed *Nick Knight*, a TV movie designed to work as the pilot for a series, in which the titular police detective was a centuries-old vampire, played by rock singer Rick Springfield, policing the streets of Los Angeles to atone for his own past crimes. The idea languished in limbo for three years, until it was resurrected as a Canadian-made series entitled *Forever Knight*, with the Welsh-born actor Geraint Wyn Davies taking on the role of the fanged cop, forever condemned to the night shift. The show had its devoted fans, as did its hero Nick Knight, but it struggled to compete with the viewing figures of the chat shows it was scheduled against, and was cancelled after just three seasons, despite feverish lobbying from devotees.

Moonlight, another Canadian-made series set in LA, suffered an even more premature end, and has been the subject of a fittingly frenzied campaign calling for its return. In this case, the undead hero is a private investigator named Mick St John, played by the bestubbled Australian actor Alex O'Loughlin. Critics were divided, many dismissing the show as corny and pedestrian, but most agreed that O'Loughlin made a spirited, sexy vampire, who certainly found a place in the hearts of numerous fans. It was the chaos created by the 2007 Hollywood Screenwriters' Strike that put a stake through the heart of *Moonlight* and the show was cancelled in 2008 after just sixteen episodes. Mick St John's fans fight on, however, and in *SFX* magazine's 2009 '50 Greatest Vampires' poll, he took an impressive fourth place. 'There was some serious block voting going on when it came to this guy,' observed the magazine, reasoning that his place was still justified. After all, 'If fans are avid enough to want to mobilise a voting campaign, what does it say about the guy they're voting for?'

Mick was still beaten to the punch by Angel, however, who claims third place – with or without block voting. David Boreanaz surprised some by actually topping another vampire poll, conducted by *Hello!* magazine in the summer of 2009. Editors clearly expected Robert Pattinson to take the title, describing his defeat as a 'shock result'. '*Twilight* actor Rob – who portrays enigmatic Edward Cullen in the film – might be the man of the moment,' said *Hello!*, 'but our readers clearly haven't forgotten David's turn as Angel.' While *Hello!* readers are hardly hardcore vampire fans, this perhaps makes the choice of David as their favourite bloodsucker even more significant. *Angel* was cancelled five years before they cast their votes – a long time in the fickle world of TV and celebrity. So, how to explain the readers' surprising preference? 'That eternal love,' says the actor of his character's doomed passion for Buffy, 'that thirst of being far apart and still loving each other, having that strength… I think because of that connection, people can identify with it.' It is that side of the multi-faceted Angel – the noble, star-crossed lover – that's secured him an enduring place in our collective affections.

Razor Blade Smile

Eileen Daly as Lilith Silver in *Razor Blade Smile*

'Part Seductress. Part Assassin. All Vampire.'

Fangs? Check. Cheekbones? Check. Skin-tight catsuit? Check. Swords and guns? Check. Lilith Silver – anti-heroine of the 1998 film *Razor Blade Smile* – ticks all the boxes for a post-modern vampire assassin and, as played by British scream queen Eileen Daly, was always destined for pin-up status among certain sections of the Goth fraternity. Anything but coy, raven-haired Eileen is candid about the assets that have seen her image adorn the bedroom walls of her numerous admirers. 'I'm the big tits, big bottom, tiny waist, "I'm going to eat you *aliiii-ive*" kind of girl and I enjoy it,' she purrs in her seductively fruity accent. Of course, it takes more than curves and a sexy voice to qualify as a memorable bloodsucker.

'Lilith isn't your usual vampire,' explains the actress and model of her first starring role. 'She's sexy in a girl-power way – she fights better than any man, has a heart of steel and takes nothing from anyone. She's a warrior, a millennium chick, a woman of the world [...] a modern-day Nikita who's had to learn to survive. She didn't originally choose to be a vampire, but she's certainly chosen a profession that suits her – an assassin for hire. Lilith psychologically is half-male and half-female – she has dual appeal. Men can see the female side: she's sexy, but deadly – the classic femme fatale; whereas women will recognise that untamed female sexuality and themselves be attracted to her as a woman who can deal with any situation. To put it in a nutshell – Lilith Silver rocks!'

And, while Eileen lacks the sophisticated poise of comparable undead assassins (Kate Beckinsale's Selene in *Underworld* or Anne Parillaud's Marie in *Innocent Blood*), her contagious enthusiasm lends a special charm to the buxom Lilith Silver. *Razor Blade Smile* had a budget that would barely have covered catering on *Underworld* or *Innocent Blood* (at £20,000 it's probably the cheapest UK film to ever enjoy a theatrical release). So Eileen never enjoyed the benefit of the special-effects wizardry, big-budget cinematography and stunt doubles that helped Kate and Anne look so good kicking ass and sucking blood. The fact that she had to do it all herself, just makes her performance all the more charming.

Running and fighting in high heels and a skin-tight catsuit isn't easy, but unlike the glacial Miss Beckinsale or the pouting Mademoiselle Parillaud, the pneumatic Ms Daly

Gothic pin-up Eileen Daly as the attitudinal vampire assassin, Lilith Silver.

appears to be having a whale of a time getting her teeth into the role. 'She was phenomenal,' enthuses *Razor Blade*'s director Jake West. 'I don't think there are many actresses out there who could have pulled this off – the mixture of hard physical action scenes that range from gunplay to samurai sword fights, intermingled with erotic seduction scenes, serious scenes and off-the-wall humour, required immense dedication and range.'

In addition to the numerous violent action sequences, the script also requires Lilith Silver to indulge in a fair amount of action between the sheets, and Eileen doesn't hesitate to get down-and-dirty with the best (and worst) of them. Her sex scenes show the same gutsy enthusiasm as her fight sequences – particularly the lesbian seduction, when Lilith sinks her teeth into her friend, a pretty young Goth who happens to be a vampire buff yet doesn't realise that Lilith is the real deal. 'I give her a bittersweet ending, pain and pleasure, but I don't give her eternal life because I don't like her that much,' laughs Eileen. 'She's not a contract killing. I'm just having a little fun.'

A triumph of enthusiasm and energy over expertise and experience, there's a raw rock'n'roll edge to *Razor Blade Smile* – a dose of underground pop-culture attitude that distinguishes the movie from more polished Hollywood product. In addition to featuring numerous guys with long hair and the setting of several scenes in a London Goth club, costumes come courtesy of the capital's foremost fetish designers, with jewellery culled from Black Rose, one of London's leading Goth accessory emporia. You might even say there's a little Goth DNA in the film's leading lady. A uniquely sultry vocalist (with Jezebel and the Courtesans), Eileen's also appeared in music videos for the notorious British metal band, Cradle of Filth. 'To be honest, it all tends to merge into a big pot of devilry over the years,' grins Eileen. Her credits range from soap operas (*Eastenders*) to sit-coms (*Snuff Box*), but Eileen always looks most at home in the realms of Gothic glamour. 'I loved *The Munsters* and *The Addams Family* when I was growing up,' she admits. 'I thought Morticia was wonderful. I really loved horror as a kid [...] the women were glam, voluptuous and well worth taking blood from.'

'I bet you think you know all about vampires. Believe me, you know fuck all.'

Razor Blade Smile is one of only a handful of vampire films made in the UK since the heyday of Hammer studios in the '60s. Since then, Britain's film studios have become best known for stuffy period pieces and dismal kitchen-sink dramas, something Jake West aimed to change with *Razor Blade*. 'I'm fed up with the British looking like the most socially repressed nation in the world,' he explained. 'It's time we regained a sense of cool sophistication – look at the impact the original Bond movies had [...] the UK was the style capital of the world. Hopefully, that could one day be the same again. So, if you like vampires, fetish gear, outrageous set-pieces, sex, shoot-outs and blood sucking, here's a film that doesn't hold back.'

Eileen describes the film as 'a comic book come to life, cartoon characters made flesh'. *Razor Blade* pays tribute to Hammer horror with a period prologue set in the Victorian era. But Lilith's kinky catsuit, the frequent fight scenes, and subplots involving international occult conspiracies are more reminiscent of the classic UK spy series *The Avengers*. 'It has

Razor Blade Smile
Part Seductress, Part Assassin, All Vampire

Every rose has its thorn … and Ms Daly proves she's no exception to the rule.

got a touch of that,' says Eileen. 'It's very '60s influenced. The film's a love story, but it's got crime and horror and a kind of female James Bond side to it too. It'll put a smile on your face. My character is a real babe. She's sensitive, she's got a sense of humour, but the years have turned her hard.' That sense of humour – a kind of bawdy irreverence – is what separates Lilith from fellow fanged femmes like Selene and Marie more than anything.

Eileen's performance is perhaps most resonant of a '60s British institution she doesn't mention – the 1966 comedy *Carry On Screaming!* One of the immensely popular series of *Carry On…* movies, this film parodies Hammer's horror films of the same era. Fenella Fielding plays the film's seductive villainess Valeria Watt, representing something of an unsung Goth heroine in the role. While the demure Valeria would never stoop to the kind of martial arts mayhem that characterises *Razor Blade*, when it comes to seduction, the voluptuous Lady Watt smoulders (in one scene quite literally) with an identical charge of velvet menace to Lilith Silver.

'It's quite tongue-in-cheek, doesn't take itself too seriously,' concludes Eileen. 'It's not proper horror, but it is kinda sexy. And I think women can appreciate that as well as men, because the roles I play don't objectify you as a dumb sex symbol; they show women as being strong, intelligent and dominant. With low-budget films like the ones I've made, special effects don't take over. It's not Francis Ford Coppola's *Dracula*. But, come to think of it, that was totally boring.' While a legion of Gary Oldman fans might disagree, it's certainly true that *Razor Blade* has bloody buckets of sleazy vim and camp vigour, due in no small part to her feisty performance in the lead role. Eileen's secret? 'Everybody's got that demon inside,' she grins, 'and mine comes out in my work.'

Buffy the Vampire Slayer

James Marsters as Spike in *Buffy the Vampire Slayer*

'What is it about dangerous women?'

Spike makes for an unlikely contender for sexiest creature of the night. In contrast to the castle-dwelling cliché, he sports a harsh, swept-back mop of peroxide locks instead of traditional midnight-black. While the classic vampire has the deep, mannered delivery of a sinister aristocrat and an iron will to match, Spike speaks in a bastardised Cockney accent – with frequent use of colourful slang – and cheerfully changes his mind at the drop of a hat. He's an irresponsible thug with a strong streak of sentimentality, matched by an insatiable appetite for alcohol and violence; a wisecracking leather-clad punk who gets his kicks from the suffering of others. 'I'm a psychopath, but I don't have a problem with that,' says the actor James Marsters of his role as Spike. Yet for many fans, Spike was still sex on legs – the coolest thing to come out of the immensely popular TV series *Buffy the Vampire Slayer*.

However unorthodox, something about Spike really caught the imagination of vampire aficionados everywhere, keeping a building legion of *Buffy* fans glued to their TV sets for the duration of the show's seven-season run, between 1997 and 2003. (Spike actually debuted in 'School Hard', the third episode of the second season.) In many respects a soap opera, *Buffy*'s longevity demanded the characters go through major changes in order to keep the dynamic fresh. Many of the main protagonists shift from villain to hero, or vice versa – and few more so than Spike, who transformed from psychopathic maverick, to tortured invalid, to love-struck loser, to reluctant hero. 'Tough guy Spike was always the funnest… I'm very bad – I love it,' said James Marsters of the ever-evolving role. 'I mean, they only let Spike be bad for three episodes, then they put him in a wheelchair and they took his teeth out and beat him on the head and made him wear a dress… sociopaths are the best.'

Spike's popularity caught those behind the show by surprise, not least *Buffy* creator and head writer Joss Whedon, which in part explains the character's changing role in the series. Spike was never supposed to become a pin-up. But like the vampire Barnabas Collins, played by Jonathan Frid in the '60s Gothic soap *Dark Shadows*, James Marsters's

James Marsters as the anarchic undead bad-boy, Spike.

character proved too popular to kill off, whatever scriptwriters had originally intended. 'Spike came in, and I started getting fan mail, and everyone was very pleased,' recalls James of his character's debut. 'And Joss took me to one side and said, "Dude, this is not the Spike show, and it's not going to be the Spike show. You are here because we don't want to kill off a villain in every episode, so it doesn't become *Scooby Doo…*"' Whedon had his reasons for resisting Spike's spiralling popularity.

James describes Spike's huge popularity as 'an accident. The thing was, when I got on the show Joss didn't want to have sexy vampires in it. To him they were metaphors for what adolescents faced in trying to become adults, so vampires were supposed to be ugly and then dead after 48 minutes and you weren't supposed to like them. He got talked into the character of Angel by David Greenwalt, who was his partner, and then Angel just took off like wildfire, and Joss was kind of in the middle trying to deal with that, trying to maintain his theme in the face of this sexy character… and then I came along.'

'I don't exactly have a reputation for being a thinker.
I follow my blood, which doesn't exactly rush in the direction of my brain.
So I make a lot of mistakes, a lot of wrong bloody calls.'

According to Spike's background in the show, he got his name from his hobby of torturing victims with railway spikes, though the name has other overtones besides, not least those of spiked hair, though in appearance he more closely resembles the leather-clad post-punk rocker Billy Idol. (The show makes joking reference to this, with Buffy implying it was Spike who inspired Idol's look rather than vice versa.) Spike's debatably the first major punk vampire (though some refer to the delinquent bloodsuckers in *The Lost Boys* as punks, they're as much biker trash as anything). According to Marsters, Joss Whedon's original concept of the character borrowed heavily from this particular subculture. 'The audition was for a vampire who was supposed to be patterned after the Sex Pistols, after Sid Vicious, who came from North London,' said the actor. 'So, I didn't know that specific accent, but I was lucky enough to be doing a play with a man from North London.'

Asked to explain Spike's unique appeal, James affected a Sid Vicious accent. 'In the words of Sid Vicious,' the actor drawled sarcastically, '"Girls love me 'cause I've got a nice face and a good figure."' On a more serious note, he added: 'Women enjoy the potency of Spike. But if a man is bad, he will be bad to you.' Bassist for the legendary Sex Pistols, Sid had little musical talent to speak of, but embodied punk's deliberately ugly ethos of self-destructive confrontation and anti-fashion. A scrawny misfit who liked a fight with an insatiable appetite for drugs, Vicious died of an overdose in 1979 while on parole under suspicion of the murder of his girlfriend Nancy Spungen. Despite, or more likely because of, the squalor surrounding his life and death, Sid became an icon, punk's nihilistic poster-boy.

During the 1998 episode of *Buffy*, entitled 'Lovers Walk', Spike sings the Frank Sinatra song, 'My Way', infamously covered by Sid Vicious, though the version that runs

Spike's tempestuous relationship with Buffy (Sarah Michelle Gellar – with blonde hair) provided some of the show's darkest storylines.

over the end of the show is taken from the 1986 biopic *Sid and Nancy* and performed by Gary Oldman, who plays Sid in the film. (Oldman, of course, went on to play Dracula in *Bram Stoker's Dracula*.) Spike and his childlike but sadistic vampire belle Drusilla were often identified as *Buffy's* own 'Sid and Nancy'. James Marsters observes that Spike 'is a sadist and he is never happier than when he is hurting people or killing people, but he is truly, sincerely, deeply in love with Drusilla.' The relationship between the psychopathic couple helped characterise Spike in his early appearances in the series, his tender devotion to Drusilla contrasting with his casual brutality in other situations.

'It is in the contrast between the fact that they don't have souls and seem to be pure evil, and they also seem to have this incredible love that is even deeper than anything we may be able to understand,' says the actor of the definitively dysfunctional relationship shared by Spike and Dru. 'In season two you see both that love set up very clearly and then completely ripped apart. So you're able to explore two characters who might have just been Frankenstein villains, and explore revenge, betrayal – everything that happens when love is not clean – and so it ended up having me just lovelorn and quite pots.' The disintegration of Spike's relationship with Drusilla heralded the beginning of a string

Spike would go on to guest in Buffy*'s sister show,* Angel.

of ordeals for his character, almost as if the scriptwriters were deliberately testing, even torturing, the character. Which perhaps they were…

Redemption, particularly redemption through suffering, is a central theme running throughout *Buffy the Vampire Slayer*, which has always been conceived by Joss Whedon as an inherently moral show. And it's particularly pertinent in the case of Spike, as Whedon seems to have felt that there was a danger of the audience being seduced by the show's cocky punk vampire. Originally created as a casual embodiment of evil, Spike now looked set to slip his leash. 'When I auditioned for the character I didn't have blonde hair and the wonderful make-up department hadn't gotten hold of me, so I looked fairly pedestrian and he didn't really expect the character to have the visual pop that it did,' recalls James. 'So he ended up really not wanting to unleash that character. Immediately after they decided not to kill Spike off they put him in a wheelchair, and after that they put a chip in his head. It was a constant – I felt – thing of "How do we not let Spike ruin our theme?"'

Addressing a range of significant emotional themes beneath its plot of high-school politics and supernatural action, *Buffy the Vampire Slayer* is a show that's developed genuine cult appeal. But its mainstream success still rests on the sharp dialogue, cool pop-cultural references (Spike's punk credentials included), and wry comedy. Spike was popular because he was one of the funniest characters, delivering some of the show's best lines in his own inimitable fashion. The danger, from an ethical point of view, was that the audience was starting to laugh with Spike, watching as he inflicted act after act of senseless brutality upon his victims. Scriptwriters responded by making the character increasingly impotent – even pathetic – in an attempt to dilute Spike's cocksure charisma.

One obvious example is Spike's background, which is revealed throughout the series, and its spin-off *Angel*. While we learn early on that Spike was known as 'William the Bloody' when he was mortal, we later discover it was because he was a poet whose verse was widely regarded as 'bloody awful'. An effete Victorian mother's boy, he is bitten by Drusilla in 1880. William converts his beloved mother, only to stake her when she turns into a monster. Alone, Spike becomes besotted by Drusilla, adopting Angel, then going through his own monstrous period, as his undead mentor, the trio becoming among the most infamously cruel bloodsuckers of the age. Spike's pathetic past life serves to generate a little sympathy for the character, as well as explaining why he may have overcompensated as a vampire, becoming hip and brutal beyond the grave as a reaction to his mousy, ineffectual nature while still alive.

> 'Love isn't brains, children – it's blood, blood screaming inside you to work its will. I may be love's bitch, but at least I'm man enough to admit it.'

By season four, a chip implanted in his head makes it impossible for him to attack anyone at all, leaving Spike defenceless and suicidal, and eventually forcing him to throw in his lot with Buffy and her demon-hunting friends. To his horror, in the following season, Spike discovers that he's fallen for Buffy. James observes that Spike 'probably fell in love with Buffy when he first saw her, but didn't admit it to himself because he was already in love with Dru'. Inevitably, the course of this affair runs far from smooth, their slowly developing relationship becoming almost as abusive as the turbulent affair between Spike and Drusilla. In 'Seeing Red' – one of the show's most shocking episodes – Spike attempts to rape Buffy. 'That was the worst day of my career,' Marsters later reflected of the emotional impact the scene had upon him. 'That was just… I just about killed myself that day.'

The actor describes the later years of the character's evolution, in which sadistic Spike develops a conscience, as deeply depressing. 'I basically had to dredge up everything I'd ever felt guilty about and flagellate myself with it on a daily basis,' he said. 'No psychologist will tell you that acting is healthy!' It is Marsters's dedication to the part and Spike's evolution from sexy, vicious villain to tormented anti-hero that makes the character so very compelling – irresistible for many viewers. 'Spike makes our top ten because he represents the ultimate female fantasy,' writes *Times* journalist Francesca Steele in her 'sexiest vampire' survey, 'the bad boy who abandons his evil ways because of his love for a woman (unlike Angel, who is already good when Buffy meets him). He is like the Vicomte de Valmont in *Dangerous Liaisons*; Mr Big in *Sex and the City*; Danny Zuko in *Grease* (just a bit more sinister and with tighter leather).'

Of course, to be redeemed, somebody has to be reprehensible to begin with – and few come more dastardly than the devil-may-care Spike of *Buffy*'s early episodes. 'If you're going to seriously redeem a character like Spike, who is a mass murderer, then he's going to have to go through a real journey,' observes James. Yet, throughout the series, there are pressures for Spike to return to his old demonic self, from not only Drusilla, but even Buffy – and, truth be told, many of the show's fans. 'I always like strutting and swinging and brawling,' confesses the actor himself. 'That is fabulous to play. That will never get old for the actor.' Or, truth be told, the audience. While some of James Marsters's most powerful scenes result from his painful attempt to reconnect with his humanity, Spike's allure still harks back to his anarchic charisma as a casual killer, the undead wildcard that cuts a bloody, chaotic swathe through *Buffy*'s moralistic world with a disarming smirk, a homicidal lunatic with a heart of gold.

From Dusk Till Dawn

Salma Hayek as Santanico Pandemonium
in *From Dusk Till Dawn*

'How far can too far go?'

And now, for your viewing pleasure,' announces Razor Charlie, the grizzled master of ceremonies and barman at tough Mexican strip joint, the Titty Twister. 'The mistress of the macabre. The epitome of evil. The most sinister woman to dance on the face of the earth. Lowly dogs, get on your knees, bow your heads and worship at the feet of Santanico Pandemonium!' The routine that follows is enough to silence even the rowdy patrons of the Titty Twister, a rough crowd of brawling bikers and hard-drinking truckers. Clad in the briefest of burgundy bikinis, a curvaceous Hispanic siren appears. A huge albino python draped across her shoulders, she sways and undulates in time to the slow, sensuous Latin-flavoured guitar of the house band, Tito and Tarantula.

Of course, Santanico wouldn't be getting so much as a mention here if she wasn't also undead. But with this sizzling routine, impossibly sultry actress Salma Hayek earned herself a special place in the hearts of many horror fans. After a few smouldering moments, however, Santanico reveals her true colours.

'The fact that she subsequently transforms into a hideous monster and bites a huge chunk off Quentin Tarantino's neck has done little to diminish her appeal as one of the sexiest vampires of all time,' notes the *Times'* reviewer. The scene represents a pivotal point in *From Dusk Till Dawn*, where all hell literally breaks loose. The movie takes a radical new direction, shifting gear from a conventional crime thriller into a gloriously gory, demented supernatural action flick. It's a Tex-Mex-style blend, where the prime meat of the film's gritty opening collides with an eye-watering dash of exotic attitude. An acquired taste perhaps – some fans were thrown off balance or even alienated by the contrasting elements – though there can be little doubt that the red-hot sauce Salma Hayek's performance adds to the mix was enough to make many mouths water.

It's a brief appearance. After her unforgettable dance (not technically a strip, regardless of how steamy it becomes), Santanico bites Tarantino's character and only gets to speak twice more – just enough to taunt her next victim. However that victim, played by George Clooney, successfully turns the tables on the beguiling bloodsucker, shooting the

Mexican firecracker Salma Hayek as the vampire queen, Santanico Pandemonium.

chain on a chandelier so that it comes tumbling down to lethally pinion Santanico to the floor. Clooney plays Seth Gecko, an escaped armed robber, and Tarantino his brother Richie, a violent sex criminal.

Quentin Tarantino wrote the script, but decided to yield the director's chair to his friend Robert Rodriguez, in order to concentrate on his acting duties. At the time, Tarantino was Hollywood's most celebrated *enfant terrible*, thanks to the success of *Pulp Fiction* (1994), while Rodriguez was enjoying a reputation as one of the most exciting new directors, courtesy of his two innovative, violent action flicks, *El Mariachi* (1992) and *Desperado* (1995). The duo bonded over a shared love of low-budget genre flicks, and *From Dusk Till Dawn* is peppered with references to other movies, paying homage to cult entertainment. The title itself is inspired by low-budget cinema, parodying the sign outside drive-ins and flea pits where movies ran all night.

Salma Hayek herself is often credited as a Rodriguez discovery. Though she was already well known in her native Mexico as a soap actress and had previously starred in *Desperado*, it was her show-stopping sequence in *From Dusk* that really established the Hispanic beauty on the Hollywood map. Rodriguez, recognising his star's smouldering natural charisma, didn't choreograph the dance, allowing Salma to merely respond to the music. The result was red-hot cinematic magic.

Salma's described Santanico Pandemonium as the 'most challenging part for me because it confronted me with my biggest phobia' – snakes. 'You have no idea what it was to dance with that snake [...] That's probably the biggest challenge I've ever encountered… to have to put on a bikini and dance with a snake eleven feet long and make it organic? I went to the extent that I created a relationship with this snake. In my mind, it had to have a meaning so I could go into a *trance*. I had to go to hypnosis – it was months of preparation for that one dance! And for me, it wasn't a dance, it was a ritual. I investigated snakes and I found in some cultures they represent your inner power, so it was a dance with her inner power. I was not just dancing; it had a meaning to me. That was really, really challenging.'

'Let's see if you taste as good as your brother.'

In a 1996 interview, the actress went into more detail on acquainting herself with the serpent, saying Tarantino had suggested ditching it from the script, but Rodriguez had insisted that the phallic reptile was a vital component of the scene, and suggested she tried dream therapy and meditation. 'Eventually, I could touch the snake with one finger, but I was running out of time,' she told the paper, and at the last minute, they called upon the services of 'Hollywood producer and mystic' Moctevuma Esparza. 'Moctevuma believes that fear is located in one part of the body as blocked energy. To unblock it, he hits you, then starts drawing on you with his hands. When I left his office the phobia was gone. When we came to film I actually enjoyed the dance a lot.'

She wasn't the only one. Rodriguez later joked that Tarantino always seemed to be on set whenever there was a Santanico scene to be shot. It was also suspicious, pondered the director, that Tarantino had written in a scene where Santanico pours whisky down her naked thigh and into the mouth of his character, Richie Gecko. 'Quentin wrote that scene for himself,' laughs Salma. 'George [Clooney] was complaining [...] I abuse him and call him my slave. He asked Quentin: "How come I get beaten up and you get to suck her toes?"' From a less whimsical perspective, while on the surface a slice of pure sexploitation, the scene does give *From Dusk* something of a moral centre.

In common with many Tarantino films, *From Dusk* came under fire for excessive violence, though the vamps were given green blood in an attempt to placate the censors and to focus on the gore is to miss a crucial point. Tarantino's character is thoroughly repellent, a sexual predator without any redeeming feature. Santanico, a literal female monster who preys on men, could be his mirror image. When she homes in on Richie, one can't help but applaud. 'I'm the one zeroing in on the females in the movie, and then narrowing my eyes to them with a sinister intention. She does the exact same thing to me – literally,' observes Tarantino, invoking karma at its most brutal.

Salma's erotic dance, hailed by many as the sexiest in cinema history.

As for Salma, though her turn as a snake-wrangling senorita established her as one of Hollywood's sexiest celebrities, she has never turned her back on her homeland. Now a naturalised US citizen, she's a prominent campaigner for women's and immigrants' rights. Fittingly, her character's name in *From Dusk* (appearing as 'Blonde Death' in early drafts of the script) was inspired by a Mexican movie entitled *Satánico Pandemonium*. Though Tarantino never actually saw the 1975 movie, its poster certainly left an impression on the former video-store worker – 'so bloody and ridiculous that I've never forgotten the name'. *Satánico* is a cult classic (in which a convent of nuns are tempted into sin by a rather camp Satan); one of numerous Mexican movies now being rediscovered by aficionados on DVD. Mexico has always had its own version of English-language horror, haunted by the lost, indigenous culture of the bloodthirsty Aztec empire – and *From Dusk* is no different. The film's final shot reveals the Titty Twister to be the apex of a gargantuan Aztec pyramid, linking the vampires' curse to the savage blood rites of ancient Mexico in a single twist.

Santanico's feather headdress gives her more than a touch of the exotic priestess, inspiring Rob Rodriguez to paint the actress as Itzpapalotl, the Aztec goddess known as the Obsidian Butterfly. Perhaps this fierce heritage is the key to Salma's success. 'How many times does one get to play a monster?' she mused. 'Some men have a silly theory about beautiful women – that somewhere along the line they'll turn into a monster. That movie gave them a chance to watch it happen.' And – it might be added – to learn that women can bite back.

Tom Cruise as Lestat in
Interview with the Vampire

'Drink from me and live forever.'

Anne Rice's hugely successful 1976 novel, *Interview with the Vampire*, changed the world of the undead forever. It helped establish steamy New Orleans as the home of American Gothic, as legions of fans were seduced by the authoress's vision of a shadow society of supernaturally elegant vampires, living a doomed, romantic existence in the twilight reaches of our drab, mortal world. When the cinematic adaptation of *Interview with the Vampire* finally hit the big screens in 1994, it had been languishing in development hell for decades. Expectations were high, and it wasn't to be an easy birth. Rice's novel had become a fanged cultural phenomenon, the sequels Rice subsequently penned – collectively known as *The Vampire Chronicles* – all enjoying bestseller status, bringing fresh blood to the vampire genre for a new generation. Fervent fans awaited the adaptation with trepidation. Would the film version be faithful to their beloved novel? Most importantly, would Hollywood do justice to the book's undead anti-heroes Louis and Lestat, with whom countless readers had already, almost literally, fallen in love?

Initial indications were promising. The director's chair was given to acclaimed Irish filmmaker Neil Jordan. His second film, the unorthodox 1984 werewolf picture *The Company of Wolves*, was a reverential recreation of the Gothic fairytale world of Angela Carter, whose fiction inspired it. Jordan co-wrote the script for *The Company of Wolves* with Carter, and was to collaborate with Rice in adapting *Interview with the Vampire* – all of which boded well for the film's fidelity to the novel. But when the casting for the movie's two undead leads was announced, in Neil Jordan's own words, 'all hell broke loose'. Brad Pitt was to play Louis, while the plum part of Lestat was assigned to Tom Cruise. They were two of Hollywood's most bankable stars – A-list mainstream heartthrobs, whose names were all but synonymous with box-office success, but hardly the first actors most Rice fans could have envisaged playing the brooding, beautiful bloodsuckers of *The Vampire Chronicles*.

Leading the outcry was the novelist herself, who went public with her severe reservations. 'I was particularly stunned by the casting of Cruise, who is no more my

Tom Cruise as Anne Rice's amoral vampire playboy, Lestat de Lioncourt.

vampire Lestat than Edward G. Robinson is Rhett Butler,' she said in 1992, later adding that the 'casting is just so bizarre, it's almost impossible to imagine how it's going to work.' When she first conceived of the character of Lestat, Anne imagined him as resembling the blonde, Dutch-born actor Rutger Hauer (who'd already played head vampire Lothos in *Buffy the Vampire Slayer*, the 1992 film which launched the popular TV series). As Hauer was considered too old for the part of Lestat by the time the film finally went into production, Rice herself favoured Julian Sands. But producers rejected the respected English actor as insufficiently commercial (in 1992 Sands played the melancholy vampire Alex in the dreamy cult flick *Tale of a Vampire*). In a prospect calculated to get fans salivating, rumour also connected Johnny Depp with the role.

But, whatever the opinions of the authoress or her fans, the producers of *Interview with the Vampire* were adamant, and the film went into production with Cruise and Pitt heading the cast. It's worth noting that, at this point, Cruise had yet to earn his eccentric reputation. Neither had he gone public with his advocacy of Scientology. And so, objections centred on the image Cruise – and to a lesser extent Pitt – had as clean-cut Hollywood hunks, of a wholesomeness wholly at odds with the dark and cultured, charismatic yet twisted characters at the core of Anne Rice's *Vampire Chronicles*. For his part, Tom pointed out that this wasn't the first time he'd ruffled a few feathers in pursuit of his chosen role: 'I've had that happen to me before on other movies, although on a smaller scale. With *Born on the Fourth of July* and with *Rain Man* there was controversy, too. Now people view those choices as successes, but before, they were saying, "Why is he choosing to do these roles?" Or, "Why did they cast Tom Cruise?"'

Neil Jordan went so far as to suggest that casting such high-profile movie idols might help the film get closer to the essence of Rice's creatures of the night. 'My feeling, having cast Brad and Tom was basically, in a strange way, the world of a vampire is not that different from the world of a massive Hollywood star,' said the director. 'You're kind of kept from the harsh daylight; you live in a strange kind of seclusion. Every time you emerge, a strange ripple runs through people. The effects these characters have, the way Anne describes them in the book was like that. Lestat would enter a room, and an invisible stone had dropped into a pool. To me, it was an interesting metaphor – star as vampire, vampire as star. As well as that, they're eternally youthful – condemned to be eternally youthful in a way.'

There were more obvious obstacles to casting Tom Cruise as Lestat, however. Anne Rice describes her anti-hero as tall and blonde; the dark-haired Cruise is not noted for his height. Tricks could be employed to increase Tom's stature on camera, while make-up effects could alter the actor's appearance – a process that sources suggest took over three hours. So as not to diminish the impact of his undead appearance, Cruise had tunnels built, allowing him to travel to the set unseen. To complete his preparation for the predatory part, the actor watched videos of lions devouring their prey. 'I remember being very nervous about taking on Lestat,' confessed Cruise. 'You know, when you read *Interview with the Vampire*, there are hints as to who Lestat is. But you hear it all from Louis's viewpoint. Lestat's a very difficult role, because he is an incredibly internalised

Lestat introduces Louis (played by Brad Pitt) to the immoral pleasures of immortality.

character and has a wonderful sense of wit. Even in his darkest moment of pain, he is still very witty!'

The preparation paid off. Both critics and audiences were impressed by the actor's performance, not least Anne Rice herself, who was even more public and effusive in her praise for Cruise's performance after seeing the film than she had been in her previous scepticism. 'From the moment he appeared, Tom was Lestat for me,' enthused the authoress. 'He has the immense physical and moral presence; he was defiant and yet never without conscience; he was beautiful beyond description yet compelled to do cruel things. The sheer beauty of Tom was dazzling, but the polish of his acting, his flawless plunge into the Lestat persona, his ability to speak rather boldly poetic lines, and speak them with seeming ease and conviction were exhilarating and uplifting.'

No doubt the success of Francis Ford Coppola's blockbuster *Bram Stoker's Dracula* two years before encouraged producers to finally give the green light to a big-budget, big-screen version of Rice's bloodsucker epic. After *Dracula*, *Interview with the Vampire* must surely be the most influential vampire novel ever written, though it certainly has

competition. Sheridan Le Fanu's *Carmilla* and *The Vampyre* by Dr John Polidori both had a substantial impact on the realms of the undead in pop culture. But both are nineteenth-century novellas, now little read except by dedicated devotees of Gothic literature, while *The Vampire Chronicles* have sold over 80 million copies worldwide over the past 30-odd years. *Carmilla* has been adapted for the big screen numerous times (several of which are covered in these pages), but Dr Polidori's tale has had a far more subtle impact upon cinematic bloodsuckers.

Entertainment Weekly asked Anne Rice recently what was unique about her vision of vampires. 'Their glamour,' responded the authoress. 'What I thought to do with Louis and Lestat was make them very beautiful and very seductive and very appealing. I thought to myself, "Why should this supernatural being be repulsive? Why should he be feral like Dracula? What if he was more like a dark angel?" It was kind if a radical idea. And now, 30 years later, no one would even question vampires being beautiful and magnetic.' Yet, as anybody familiar with the 'Vampyre' created by ill-fated physician Polidori could tell you, the idea of glamorous vampires was already over 150 years old when Rice wrote *Interview with the Vampire*.

'I like to do it. I enjoy it. Take your aesthetes, taste purer things; kill them swiftly, if you will, but do it. For do not doubt, you are a killer, Louis.'

The authoress's book is, nevertheless, a formidable achievement. *Entertainment Weekly* credit Lestat, the charismatic character she first introduced in the novel, as number one in their poll of the '20 Greatest Vampires'. 'Without Lestat there would be no *Twilight*,' acclaims the magazine. 'Foppishly charming, endearingly tortured, and always trendy no matter what the century, he became the template for all culturally relevant vampires since.' The same description might equally apply to Lord Ruthven, undead anti-hero of *The Vampyre*, first published in 1819. While the vampire of authentic medieval folklore had traditionally been a foul-smelling, repellent peasant, Polidori based his own vampire on his glamorous, aristocratic ex-employer, Lord Byron. 'I've always been fascinated by the vampire, the elegant yet evil Byronic figure,' admits Anne Rice. 'It's easy to say it's a metaphor for the outsider, the predator – anyone who feels freakish or monstrous or out of step, but appears normal.'

The quintessential scandalous Romantic poet – the celebrity as outcast – Lord Byron drank and womanised his way across Europe, before dying fashionably young in 1824. Broodingly handsome, sarcastically witty, and deliciously wicked, the moody aristocrat Byron was infamously branded 'mad, bad and dangerous to know' by one of his discarded conquests. In the process, he unwittingly became the original blueprint for the beguiling, blue-blooded bloodsucker when Polidori used him as the model for the dashing but

Louis wreaks flaming vengeance on the Théâtre des Vampires for the killing of his 'daughter', Claudia.

deadly Lord Ruthven. All but forgotten today, the character of Ruthven became a minor sensation in his own era, inspiring a vogue for vampire plays in Paris during the early 1800s – reminiscent of the seductively sinister Théâtre des Vampires that features in *Interview with the Vampire*. Anne Rice claims not to have heard of the real-life Parisian vampire shows of the nineteenth century before she invented her fictional version, but the similarities are striking. Similarly, even if Lestat wasn't a conscious reincarnation of Polidori's Byronic bloodsucker, Lord Ruthven, he does at least belong to the same, tainted aristocratic bloodline.

In *Interview with the Vampire*, Lestat is part of an undead double act, alongside Louis de Pointe du Lac, the Louisiana plantation owner that he bites to become his companion in immortality. If Lestat represents the amoral, sarcastic devil-may-care charm of the Byronic personality, Louis embodies the more troubled, self-destructive aspects. Tormented by grief in life (for the death of his brother in the book, the loss of his wife and child in the film), once undead, Louis becomes similarly tortured by his identity as a predator, destined to live off the blood of innocents to sustain his own life, constantly at war with his own nature. 'Of course, he loves Louis,' observes Tom Cruise of his character's relationship with Louis. 'He made Louis. He chose Louis. And to Lestat, he gave him the greatest gift ever. But Louis does not really recognise what Lestat has given him until close to the end of the movie, and he never truly appreciates what he's given him.'

As much as Lestat and Louis are bound together in an unholy partnership, there is also friction between the two – and even an element of rivalry. Louis is complicit in Lestat's attempted murder by Claudia, the little girl Lestat converts to be Louis's companion. There is also rivalry between the two vampires for the attention and sympathy of the reader. *Interview with the Vampire* is written from Louis's perspective, and one suspects that Rice began intending the more humane vampire to be her hero. But somehow the devilish Lestat steals our, and ultimately Rice's, affections. When she finally penned a follow-up to *Interview with the Vampire* in 1985, it was entitled *The Vampire Lestat*, while in 1988, when devotees of her *Vampire Chronicles* decided to start an official society, it was dubbed the Vampire Lestat Fan Club. He's simply more fun than the gloomy, worthy Louis – not least as played by Tom Cruise, who evidently relished sinking his teeth into his role, invariably stealing one scene after another from the somewhat moribund Brad Pitt.

If Anne Rice didn't quite invent the glamorous vampire in *Interview with the Vampire*, then the novel's powerful homoerotic overtones certainly seemed fresh back when her novel was first published in the '70s. 'Once Louis and Lestat become vampires, they're left squabbling through eternity in a way,' observes Neil Jordan, making them sound every inch the bitchy gay couple of cliché. 'One gay bookshop, Unicorn Books in West Hollywood, told this author that all its best-selling titles for a period during 1991 were vampire titles, with Anne Rice topping the list,' wrote David J. Skal in *The Monster Show*. 'In the three novels of her *Vampire Chronicles* series to date, Rice spins a seductive, evocative myth of gender transcendence among the living dead, consciously seeking a gay resonance.' (There were ten official volumes in the series by the time she published the last novel in 2003.)

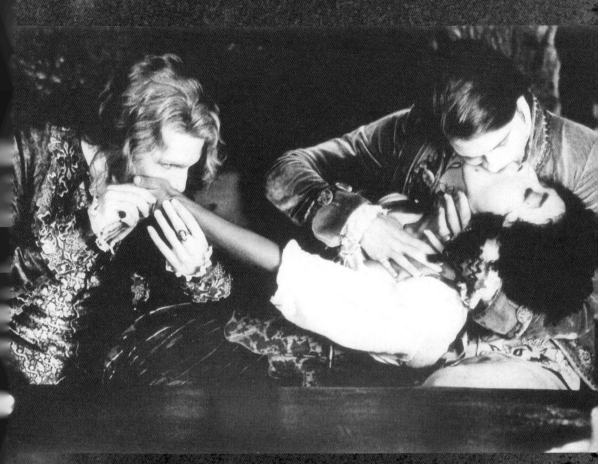

Lestat and Louis share a meal.

So, was Anne Rice the first to bring vampires out of the coffin, as it were? While Lord Ruthven exclusively targeted damsels in distress in *The Vampyre*, his inspiration, Lord Byron, was plagued by rumours of bisexuality. *Carmilla* heaves with as many lesbian overtones as might feasibly be published without fear of sanction in 1872. As we shall see, Hollywood's *Dracula's Daughter* (which Rice has credited as an influence) also baited the censors with Sapphic subtexts in 1936, while big-screen adaptations of *Carmilla* made the novella's sexual elements increasingly explicit – starting with *Blood and Roses* in 1960 – to the point that lipstick lesbian vampirism had become something of a cliché by the '70s. Male homosexuality, on the other hand, has proven a more stubborn vampiric taboo.

Producers of the original Hollywood *Dracula* in 1931 recognised the sexual subtext of the vampire's kiss, and insisted male vampires bite only female victims. In 1960, Britain's Hammer studios followed up the success of their 1958 *Dracula* with *Brides of Dracula*. Its lead vampire, Baron Meinster is an effete blonde aristocrat somewhat reminiscent of Lestat. David Peel, the actor playing the Baron, endured sniggering innuendos concerning his sexuality from the UK tabloid press during the film's publicity campaign. In 1967,

Roman Polanski's *Dance of the Vampires* featured a gay blonde vampire called Herbert – who might be seen as a crude parody foreshadowing Lestat – though like the rest of the film, this is chiefly played for cheap laughs. In 1969, *Does Dracula Really Suck?* was released, the first of a sporadic series of gay vampire porn flicks. But in terms of serious treatments of same-sex male relationships in vampire literature and film, *Interview with the Vampire* represented a milestone as both a book and a film. It illustrated, if nothing else, that female vampire fans could find idealised male relationships just as titillating as many males found the lesbian equivalent.

'Evil is a point of view. God kills indiscriminately, and so shall we. For no creatures under God are as we are: none so like him as ourselves'

When *Interview with the Vampire* debuted, it was a sign of increasingly enlightened attitudes that a number criticisms focused on the film's homosexual subtext not being overt enough. In response to one critic who asked why the lead characters had to be vampires instead of just homosexual, Anne Rice angrily wrote, 'The gays are us… There is no disguise. Gay allegory doesn't exist apart from moral allegory for everyone.' Tom Cruise didn't duck the homosexual overtones of the story in interview, instead agreeing with Anne that a purely homosexual interpretation misses the point. 'I think that really limits what the book is about and what the characters stand for,' said the actor. 'They are vampires. It's very important to understand that. There is an eroticism. But I think if someone is a homosexual, to them it will be homoerotic. And if they're not homosexual, it will be heteroerotic.'

'The book is what the book is to whoever reads it,' adds the actor. 'To my eye, that's what makes it sensual. You're dealing with creatures that seem human, that have human complexities, and yet are very much not human. Lestat is a vampire. He is immortal. He feeds off humans. It is the first time that you are seeing what humans would call a monster's viewpoint of life. It is the viewpoint of the lion, not Bambi. And the thing is that Louis wants to be Bambi! And Lestat says, "We are lions now." He makes Louis a lion.' 'I think one of the genius qualities to the film is that Neil Jordan was so bold in pursuing that theme,' said Anne Rice of the director's full-blooded approach to the story, 'that they are really evil, they do take life and they do drink blood in order to survive, and they're kind of stuck with it.'

In 1998, after decades of rejecting religion, Anne Rice returned to the fold of the Catholic Church, announcing in 2002 that she would henceforth dedicate her writing career to Christ. It spelled the end for her *Vampire Chronicles* and left the authoress with the difficult task of reassuring her new potential Christian readership, many of whom had been vigorous in condemning exactly the sort of fiction that had made her wealthy. 'If I had it to do over again, I would not use the word "vampire" in my novels,' she declared in a 2007 'Essay on Earlier Works'. 'As I look back on it, I have to say that the use of this word did indeed bring me popular attention, but it brought me that attention at a dreadful price.' While Rice remains on the liberal end of Catholicism, condemning homophobia, her new faith found her in some strange company in 2008 – conducting a cosy radio chat with the evangelist Dr James Dobson, founder of Focus on the Family. In 2005, the doctor and his organisation hit the headlines for condemning the cartoon character Spongebob Squarepants as homosexual propaganda. The mind boggles as to what he would make of the vampire Lestat…

Tom Cruise's religious affairs have been the source of even greater media attention. He appears to have become involved with Scientology previous to shooting *Interview with the Vampire*, though the association has only become the source of scandal in recent years. Scientologists vigorously dispute that their organisation is a cult, but the actor's increasingly high-profile support for the controversial movement and its unorthodox beliefs have certainly tarnished Cruise's reputation in the eyes of many fans. A bizarre, manic appearance on *The Oprah Winfrey Show* in 2005 further fuelled the star's building reputation for disturbingly erratic behaviour.

In her recent 'Top 10 Sexiest Vampires' feature for the *Times*, journalist Francesca Steele gives her number one spot to Brad Pitt as Louis in *Interview with the Vampire*. 'Louis's brand of handsome, brooding anguish is the reason why vampires play on our heartstrings in a way that zombies and werewolves never could,' sighs Steele. Lestat is reduced to the status of an also-ran. 'We know it's not quite fair to let real life affect our film judgement (and Cruise is actually brilliant as Lestat), but we can't quite see him as sexy since we saw that YouTube video of an oddly hyper Tom cackling hysterically about his spiritual enlightenment,' explains the journalist. It isn't fair to allow our judgements about an actor's lifestyle to cloud our assessment of their work, and in *Interview with the Vampire*, Cruise's sparklingly acid Lestat not only outshines Pitt's rather pedestrian Louis, but puts most rival vampires in the shade.

The journalist Ingrid Sischy asked Cruise to answer questions in character as Lestat. How did he feel about Louis revealing his life story? 'I certainly felt betrayed hearing the story that I lived for centuries. I try not to torture myself for my own mistakes. To hear how he misunderstood my own capacity to love, to be alive in many ways, I found not so surprising. But I don't know, maybe I'm just an endless romantic, hoping that one day it will change, or the full realisation of what I have given to the world will be recognised.' And how does he avoid torturing himself with such thoughts? 'I torture others,' laughs Cruise's Lestat. And what of Louis? 'Did you not fall in love with Louis's beautiful suffering human heart that everyone was so seduced by? Part of who we are, vampires I mean, is our beauty. To be beautiful. To live forever. To be powerful. I know it sounds so vain, but we do need something to hide the pain and the loneliness, don't we?'

Bram Stoker's Dracula

Gary Oldman as Dracula in
Bram Stoker's Dracula

'Love Never Dies.'

What if your lover would wait for you, not just days, weeks or months, but for centuries? What if they were consumed by a passion so intense, it transcended not only countless years and hundreds of miles, but the very laws of God? These are the questions at the heart of *Bram Stoker's Dracula*, director Francis Ford Coppola's 1992 Gothic romance, in which Gary Oldman embodies the immortal Count as not just one of myth's greatest monsters, but one of history's greatest lovers. It is a tribute to Oldman's performance that he successfully captures both aspects of the character, in a role that demands he communicates the Count's inner conflict – not only in the familiar form of the dapper aristocrat, but in a series of bizarre incarnations. 'Here's how sexy Oldman is in Francis Ford Coppola's opus,' observes Hollywood.com in their 'Top 10 Sexiest Vampires' list: 'Even disguised as a creepy mist, he turns women on.'

He may not quite 'turn women on' as a swarm of rats tumbling to the floor, or the bestial half-wolf creature that ravishes Lucy, but Oldman does successfully create a coherent, believable character, despite his numerous supernatural transformations throughout the film – many of them requiring him to act while heavily made-up. 'What I thought was interesting about the script is that it deals with earthbound emotions and fears that we all understand and can relate to,' said Gary Oldman of what first drew him to take the part. 'We understand the joys of love and the pain that comes with love and it works on all of those levels and that's why it intrigues me. It was […] not just a one-dimensional monster.'

Perhaps the least savoury of the Count's numerous incarnations is as the ancient master of Castle Dracula early in the film – his white hair in a bizarre, Baroque style, his skin parchment-pale with age, literally desiccated for lack of life-giving blood. In this incarnation, the Count is horribly creepy, his ornate gown trailing behind him like some monstrous tail. While much vampire lore insists that the undead cast no shadow, Coppola has the Count's shadow operate almost independently of its owner – an occult presence that menaces his anxious guest Jonathan Harker. This creative use of shadow

Gary Oldman, arguably the big screen's most romantic interpretation of the Count.

to communicate supernatural terror clearly references *Nosferatu*, the first unofficial film adaptation of *Dracula*, made in 1922.

Coppola makes reference to several other incarnations of the Count throughout the film, though as its title suggests, the director was keen to emphasise his film's fidelity to the original 1897 novel. Certainly, his depiction of Dracula gradually growing younger as he taps into the blood supply of an unsuspecting British Empire recreates a key theme of the book often forgotten in other adaptations. Another film to feature this was the 1970 B-movie *Count Dracula*, by the Spanish cult director Jess Franco. Franco's declaration that he intended to film the book faithfully convinced Christopher Lee to take the title role, even though Lee had publicly stated he was tired of playing the Count. *Count Dracula* isn't as faithful as Franco claims, though it does at least depict Dracula as Bram Stoker describes him – a grey-haired, moustachioed aristocrat. By way of contrast, there is no precedent in the text for the decrepit creature with bizarrely bouffant hair, who Coppola features in his version.

The incarnation that Gary Oldman's Count adopts for most of the film is of a dashing Victorian gentleman, dapper in a grey suit and top hat, distinguished only from the fashionable London crowds that surround him by his long, chestnut hair, dark glasses and thick Eastern-European accent. It's enough to lend him a heady aura of exoticism, making it easy to see why Mina Harker, as played by Winona Ryder, finds the Count difficult to resist. His manners are impeccable, though not so opaque as to conceal a deeply sensitive soul beneath the façade, particularly when speaking on the subject of his beloved mother country. There is also something unnerving and enigmatic about this foreign aristocrat. 'I have tried to play him as rather like Raphael – a fallen angel,' says Oldman. 'He's torn […] a tortured soul. I don't play him out-and-out as an evil character. There's all that in there too – it's a delicious cocktail.' 'He is unlike any man,' offers Winona. 'He is mysterious and he's dangerous. He's very sexual – he's very attractive in that dangerous way,' the actress adds with a giggle.

'I give you life eternal. Everlasting love. The power of the storm. And the beasts of the earth. Walk with me to be my loving wife, forever.'

That danger builds as their relationship blossoms, the ever-growing threat only seeming to intensify the forbidden passion between Dracula and the object of his unholy desire. It is this that exposes the vulnerable, human side to Oldman's ancient monster. In contrast with most vampires, he not only declines to use his formidable supernatural powers to seduce his victim, but when the opportunity presents itself to make Mina his bride, the tearful Count cannot bring himself to do it. Here, the tables almost turn. Mina must suck the blood from a cut Dracula has made in his naked chest in order to join him in accursed immortality. While the conflicted Count tries weakly to push

Dracula embraces his long-lost love, Princess Elisabeta, reincarnated as Mina (played by Winona Ryder).

Mina attempts to join the Count in immortality in one of the film's most sexually-charged scenes.

her away, Winona Ryder's Mina almost forces herself upon him, sucking eagerly at his tainted blood in her own blasphemous fervour, insensate to everything but her desire to be possessed by her lover. 'This thing with Dracula is something completely different – it's uncontrollable,' explained the actress. Dracula's literal inhumanity, even the fact that he murdered her best friend, Lucy, is ignored – nothing matters to Mina but being consumed by their shared passion.

The romance between Mina and the Count remains at the heart of *Bram Stoker's Dracula* – something that distinguishes it from its source material. In Stoker's original novel, Dracula is anything but a romantic figure. He is more of a supernatural sex criminal. If he targets Mina for any reason other than naked bloodlust, it is to avenge himself upon the vampire-hunters for staking his first English victim, Lucy Westenra. In his film, Coppola creates a backstory for Dracula that barely pays lip service to Stoker's book. In the movie's prologue, we meet Dracula while he was still alive: a medieval war hero clad in blood-red armour, crusading against the Turks on behalf of the Church. When word gets back to his castle, inaccurately stating that Dracula has died in battle, his distraught bride commits suicide. Outraged and inconsolable at the death of his beloved, Dracula curses the God he feels has betrayed him, inviting the curse that will grant him unholy immortality.

The character played by Oldman in the prologue is Vlad III, Prince of Wallachia, a real Romanian warlord of the fifteenth century. 'Francis gave everybody little tasks to get into their character,' said Gary of the director's unorthodox preparation for *Bram Stoker's Dracula*. 'He'd send them off to do balloon bonding, or Keanu [Reeves, who plays Jonathan Harker] would go and ride horses. I said, "What do I do? I'm 400 years old and I'm dead!" So I stole from the historical figure.' The real Vlad, who lived between 1431 and 1476, is perhaps better known by his nickname – the Impaler – in reference to his favourite form of execution. Impalement is a particularly slow and savage means of execution, which involves placing the victim on a tall, sharpened pole, their own bodyweight gradually forcing the point up through the victim's body. It was just one of the various forms of torture and murder that Vlad doled out, inflicted upon both his Turkish enemies and his own people during a reign that became notorious for its brutality.

Vlad's other title was Dracula, meaning 'son of the dragon' or 'son of the Devil' – a reference to his father, who took the title Vlad Dracul after being made a member of the chivalric Order of the Dragon. It wasn't until the 1970s that two US-based academics named Radu Florescu and Raymond McNally first popularised the fact that Bram Stoker had taken the name for his fictional vampire from a real historical figure. How much else Stoker borrowed from the history books for his immortal villain remains controversial. Some patriotic Romanians take great exception to the association. To them, Vlad Dracul was a national hero for his bold military campaigns against the Turks. Yet the pioneering scholarship of Florescu and McNally had a huge impact on the legacy of *Dracula*, cementing in the minds of horror aficionados an association between medieval warlord and fictitious vampire, which was only ever hinted at in Bram Stoker's 1897 novel.

Perhaps the first film to reference this link was a Turkish production, known in the West as *Dracula in Istanbul*, back in 1953. It should come as no surprise that the Turks remembered Vlad the Impaler and made the connection, as the historical 'Dracula' played the part of bloodthirsty villain in their own history books, but the film was hardly seen outside the country Vlad had terrorised. The first Western production to highlight the link was the 1973 TV movie *Dracula*, starring the craggily menacing Jack Palance in the title role. It anticipated Coppola's *Bram Stoker's Dracula* by having Palance's Count pursuing

Oldman's Dracula is a slave to both his bloodlust and his loneliness.

Lucy because she is the reincarnation of the love of his life – lost to him 400 years ago. Yet this 1973 version lacked the impact of Coppola's higher profile – and frankly superior – vision, and it was the 1992 film that firmly cemented a link between Vlad the Impaler and Bram Stoker's fictional Count in the popular imagination, inspiring a number of spin-offs and cash-ins such as the 2000 TV movie *Dark Prince* and the 2003 film *Vlad*.

Just as Francis Ford Coppola's adaptation deviates significantly from the original novel, so his version of *Dracula* takes some liberties with the historical background – as depicted in the film's dramatic prologue. In Coppola's version, Gary Oldman's Vlad is inspired to declare war on Heaven when his bride Elisabeta commits suicide by throwing herself from the castle battlements, only to be reincarnated as Mina four centuries later. Vlad the Impaler did have a wife who took her own life in this fashion in 1462, but we do not know her name, and she killed herself when the castle was being besieged by the Turks, preferring death to capture, not after being misinformed of her husband's death. Meanwhile, Vlad escaped across the mountains to fight another day. Inevitably, the historical reality is less romantic than Coppola's fantasy, and if Gary Oldman 'stole from the historical figure' in order to colour his performance, he did so very selectively. Vlad the Impaler is scarcely a romantic figure. He had numerous wives and mistresses after his first bride's demise. In one particularly horrific episode, one of them told Vlad that she was pregnant in order to try and lift his mood. The sceptical Impaler drew his sword and slit his lover open in order to prove that she was lying. However monstrous he may be, it's difficult to imagine Oldman's Dracula perpetrating such a casual act of sadistic brutality.

'I have crossed oceans of time to find you.'

Coppola picks and chooses from the life of the historical Dracula, just as he incorporates some elements of Bram Stoker's novel and abandons others, whatever the title of the film might imply. Some critics have suggested that a more accurate title for the movie would have been 'Francis Ford Coppola's Dracula', as it is his vision that makes the film unique. The director creates a stylised world that is at once recognisably Victorian and lavishly Gothic, with epic sets and arresting costumes that combine historical elegance and elements of dark fantasy. These aspects of the production were duly officially recognised, with *Bram Stoker's Dracula* winning Oscars for its costumes, sound effects, and make-up. More importantly, it proved a hit with audiences, who embraced its midnight cocktail of forbidden love and supernatural thrills, making it by some estimates the most commercially successful version of *Dracula* ever filmed.

For all this, Gary Oldman's Dracula has yet to achieve the iconic status of the classic portrayals of Christopher Lee and Bela Lugosi. His Count, borrowing the long hair and moustache of historical Vlad, has many fans, but when people think of Dracula, his image is still more reminiscent of Lee or Lugosi. Yet *Bram Stoker's Dracula* must be among the most romantic versions of the story ever told and Oldman's Prince of Darkness one of the most passionate creatures of the night – marking an accomplished performance from one of cinema's most talented actors. 'There are some loves that are eternal, that you take to the grave with you,' he said of preparing for the role. 'This guy has been searching for 400 years... I have invested a lot of what I know and what I have experienced into this part. You really want to know what love is? Read a Shakespeare sonnet. Listen to a Frank Sinatra song.' Or, as some viewers might suggest, watch *Bram Stoker's Dracula*.

Innocent Blood

Anne Parillaud as Marie in *Innocent Blood*

'A movie that goes straight for the jugular.'

We find Marie in a pensive mood at the opening of 1992's *Innocent Blood*. We also find our boyishly slender heroine stark naked. She's an independently-minded free spirit in the classic tradition of French cinematic heroines – confident, coquettish and comfortable with her own sensuality. Though the phrase *joie de vivre* is perhaps inappropriate when applied to an undead femme fatale like Marie, unlike many vampires she hasn't lost the traditional Gallic appetites for romance and good food, even if her condition now means that garlic is off the menu. The French vampire finds herself in the American city of Pittsburgh, both lonely and hungry. A newspaper headline suggests a solution to Marie's second problem, with a report of gang violence among the local Mafiosi. For our Gallic bloodsucker has standards, and will only take the lives of those deserving of her lethal talents. Her own woman – or indeed vampire – Marie has her own way of doing things, an approach that extends not only to her eating habits, but also her love life. As *Innocent Blood* unfurls, both will present problems for the film's heroine.

The French actress Anne Parillaud, who had become an international star playing the title role of a deadly female assassin in the 1990 French thriller *Nikita*, plays Marie. There are obvious parallels between the characters of Nikita and Marie. Both are sinuous killing machines, able to lull their prey with their apparent vulnerability. *Nikita* helped launch a trend for slender sex kittens who belie appearances by kicking ass (witness Kate Beckinsale in *Underworld* or Milla Jovovich in *Ultraviolet*, for example). But too often the director relies upon stunt professionals and special effects to make their femme fatales look like fearsome martial artists, resulting in post-feminist heroines who never truly convince in the fight scenes. Anne took her preparation for *Nikita* seriously, getting into character the hard way, undertaking three months of martial arts and firearms training. It went against the grain with the pacifist French actress – 'I hate guns, I hate violence, I hate judo,' she says – but paid dividends on the screen, with a character who seems plausibly lethal despite her outward fragility.

Anne felt that the nihilist Nikita got a little too far under her own skin. 'For a while

Anne Parillaud as Marie, the chic Gallic vampire with a conscience.

she was in me like a demon,' she says. 'I would do things I normally would not do. She was awkward, depressed, full of despair. But to me there was also a spiritual underline to Nikita. In a very excessive way she is a loudspeaker of the youth of society today. She destroys herself because she doesn't believe in anything on Earth.' Though she left France in the wake of *Nikita*'s international success, Anne turned down the opportunity to revisit the part for a Hollywood remake. She was, however, drawn to the role of Marie in *Innocent Blood*, despite outward similarities between the female assassin and the ethical vamp. The French actress saw elements of Marie's character – an essential loneliness, courage in the face of adversity – that appealed. 'I fell in love with Marie in *Innocent Blood* because she wasn't born a vampire; she never decided she wanted to be,' she says. 'For me, it was a parable to talk about how you deal with this problem, which is when you are different. You think or you live or you want something different from everyone else. People don't follow you, because it's scary. You are quite alone in your choices.'

The contrast between Anne Parillaud's French vampire and *Innocent Blood*'s Italian-American mobsters provides much of the film's unique flavour. The Mafiosi are arrogant, boorish macho men in the worst sense of Mediterranean cliché. In particular the Mob boss Salvatore 'The Shark' Macelli is more of a monster than Marie could ever be, the actor Robert Loggia playing him as a repellent, swaggering sharp-suited thug in a performance that stays just the right side of over-the-top. The gangsters' sexist machismo makes them particularly easy prey for the delicate Marie, whose ingenue charms and tomboyish good looks allow her to slip in under their radar. Things go wrong, however, when she bites Macelli, but fails to finish him off, potentially unleashing a plague of immortal, superpowered Mafiosi on an unsuspecting Pittsburgh. As a consequence, she finds herself teamed up with a cop named Joseph Gennaro, played by Anthony LaPaglia, who has sworn to bring Sal the Shark to justice, initially unaware that his quarry is now a vampire.

'He looked promising ... He felt promising. But his eyes were sad. So very sad. My first rule - never play with the food.'

In many respects, Gennaro represents the flipside of the negative Latino characters in Macelli's gang – he is a decent, honourable man, albeit one somewhat blinded by his vendetta with the Mob boss. Marie falls for his charms – the two share not just a desire to bring down the vile Macelli, but also a kindred sadness. The scene where she finally seduces Gennaro is hot stuff. To calm the detective, understandably nervous at getting intimate with a vampire, she invites him to handcuff her. The shot where a naked Marie bows before Gennaro, supplicating herself like an obedient slave, crackles with kinky energy. The subsequent moment when she snaps the cuffs off her wrists as if they were made of paper serves as a reminder that Marie is capable of being deadly as well as passionate and tender. Despite outward appearances, this is no prissy vampire. In killing mode her eyes glow a hellish red and her sweet French accent transforms into a low, demonic growl. She doesn't nibble demurely at her victims, but rips out their throats in showers of crimson plasma, calmly finishing the job with a shotgun blast to the face

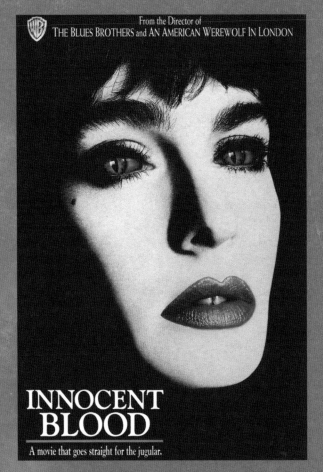

From the Director of
THE BLUES BROTHERS and AN AMERICAN WEREWOLF IN LONDON

INNOCENT BLOOD

A movie that goes straight for the jugular.

to ensure that they don't return as vampires themselves.

Innocent Blood was something of a flop upon release. In part, perhaps, because it was overshadowed by the heavily-promoted *Bram Stoker's Dracula*, which came out just two weeks later. It's also a hybrid movie – part gritty gangster flick, part romantic comedy, part full-blooded horror film – and pictures that straddle genres can prove difficult to market successfully. According to its director, John Landis, 'Critics don't like it when you fuck with genre. *An American Werewolf in London* is still called a comedy. It's not a comedy; it's a horror movie.' Landis is best known among horror fans for his 1981 werewolf film, which, despite what the director says, is still regarded by many devotees as a horror-comedy crossbreed. Like *Innocent Blood*, *An American Werewolf in London* initially enjoyed a lukewarm response, but is now widely recognised as a classic. *Innocent Blood* has yet to come in from the cold, which is a shame, as its individual elements – from the gross-out gags to the sleazy gangster subplots (it features actors who would go on to future success in award-winning TV series *The Sopranos*) – all work well together. It also features one of the cutest undead Mademoiselles in the history of vampire cinema.

The French have a rich vampiric tradition. It was a Frenchman, the clergyman and scholar Dom Antoine Augustin Calmet, who first introduced the Western world to vampires. His 1746 study, *Dissertations sur les apparitions, des anges, des démons et des esprits, et sur les revenants et vampires de Hongrie, de Boheme, de Moravie et de Silésie*, caused something of a sensation, and introduced the word 'vampire' into Western European dictionaries. Charles Baudelaire, perhaps France's greatest poet, included several vampires in *Les Fleurs du Mal*, his 1857 anthology of morbid and erotic verse, which proved so scandalous that it was prosecuted for obscenity. The Parisian conjuror Georges Méliès is widely regarded as the father of fantastic cinema, using early special effects and camera tricks to create magic on the screen. His two-minute short *Le Manoir du Diable*, in which a devil flies into the room in the form of a bat before being dispelled by a knight brandishing a cross, is sometimes cited as the first ever vampire film. It was released in 1896, the year before Bram Stoker's famous novel *Dracula* was first published.

> 'When you are alone eternally, you live for the comfort of the senses: food, sex. I'd become very selective and it was getting harder for me to find food, even living in the city. My choosiness about food cost me my lover, and without him there is no sex.'

Overall, however, French cinema – with its proud artistic tradition – has largely looked down its collective nose at horror until recent years. A few of the nation's directors and performers have turned their talents to the realms of the undead before Anne Parillaud flew the flag for French vampires in *Innocent Blood*. In 1960, the Parisian filmmaker Roger Vadim adapted the famous vampire novella *Carmilla* as *Blood and Roses*. He cast his second wife, Annette, as the film's female vampire in the oft-filmed story and, while it has much to commend it – and she is certainly a beautiful actress – her performance and *Blood and Roses* itself come across as a little anaemic and listless when compared to Hammer's adaptation, *The Vampire Lovers*. Vadim is almost as notorious for being a ladykiller as he is famous as a filmmaker, and he divorced Annette shortly after *Blood and Roses* was released. The legendary sex kitten Brigitte Bardot was his first wife, and in his memoirs he describes being discovered by Brigitte in the games room of a hotel in the company of a teenage girl. The girl was naked except for her pants and socks. 'We're playing strip pool,' he explained.

That teenage girl was Catherine Deneuve, who would in time become a French cinematic icon in her own right. She would also play a memorable vampire in the 1983 Hollywood horror movie *The Hunger*. By then Deneuve was established as the essence of enigmatic Gallic sexuality, an aloof, picture-perfect beauty who had become the face of Chanel No. 5, inspiring record sales of the perfume in the US during the '70s. In *The Hunger* she plays Miriam Blaylock, opposite rock star David Bowie as her partner John. The pair are a stylish couple in contemporary New York who also happen to be supernatural bloodsuckers. The film is a triumph of style over substance – which is simultaneously its strength and its weakness. It's a rare example of a vampire film that focuses on the myth's implications as a metaphor for the fear of ageing. John, who is starting to age fast, seeks out the help of Dr Sarah Roberts, a scientist who specialises in ageing, played by Susan Sarandon. But Dr Roberts falls under Miriam's spell, entering into an intense relationship with the sophisticated European vamp, as Bowie's character literally wastes away.

The Hunger was widely dismissed by critics of the day as vapid vampirism, the descendents of Dracula re-imagined as New York yuppies. But the film soon attained cult status, particularly amongst two distinct constituencies. The fledgling Goth movement were beguiled by the opening sequence, in which Deneuve and Bowie (a popular figure in the nascent subculture) go hunting in a New-Wave nightclub. The house band is Bauhaus, playing their 1979 song 'Bela Lugosi's Dead', a track widely regarded as the first fully-fledged Goth single. For many Goths *The Hunger* – with its stylishly overripe, amoral ambience – remains a cinematic touchstone. The film also has an iconic status in lesbian cinema, the steamy sex scene between Sarandon and Deneuve inspiring more than one female viewer to discover their own sexuality. 'That didn't start until after I did *The Hunger*,' observed Catherine Deneuve of her status as a lesbian pin-up. 'I think it was because the love scene between the women was so beautiful in *The Hunger*. I think Tony Scott, the director, made such a visually beautiful film, especially at that time, because it was a vampire story. I love vampire stories. That's why I did the movie. Women especially were taken with that movie – even more so when it came out on video. They always ask me to sign the cassette box of that video.'

There is no denying that Catherine Deneuve's performance is iconic – though perhaps more groundbreaking if you are unfamiliar with the history of vampire cinema. 'It is true that before *The Hunger*, the film image of a lesbian was always very masculine,' said Catherine of the film's impact. 'She would have to dress like a man. If there was going to be a woman who liked a woman, then she had to look like a man. *The Hunger* had a very strong image of beautiful women, so perhaps it is true. Suddenly, there was a woman looking like a woman and liking women. Yes, I showed you can be beautiful and be a lesbian. Maybe I did that.'

Or, as some individuals would have it, maybe not: 'The lesbian vampire has a long and honourable past,' according to Lindsy Van Gelder, who is credited with writing one of the first articles on lesbian chic in the *Los Angeles Times* in 1992. 'The idea of a beautiful, predatory, undead glamour-puss has been going on for some time, but it is surprising how many lesbians I've interviewed [who] mention *The Hunger* and *that* actress!'

Deneuve's Miriam Blaylock, with her potent air of aloof Gallic chic and timeless predatory sophistication, earned a place in numerous recent 'Sexiest Vampire' polls. Yet, just as Annette Vadim's Carmilla is less impressive than Ingrid Pitt in the same role in Hammer's *The Vampire Lovers*, in this author's estimation *The Hunger*'s elegant vampire villainess pales beside the stylish undead glamour puss Countess Bathory, played by the French-educated actress Delphine Seyrig in *Daughters of Darkness*, who we shall meet presently. Recent competition for the crown of France's most delectable bloodsucker has come in the form of another foreign-born femme, in the striking shape of Ukrainian actress Olga Kurylenko. In 2006's *Paris, je t'aime* – a production for which a selection of distinguished directors were invited to contribute love letters to the French capital in the form of short films – Kurylenko plays a vampire who steals the heart of an American tourist. The fact that the tourist was played by Elijah Wood (famous for his role as Frodo Baggins in *The Lord of the Rings*) and that Olga would go on to become a Bond girl in *Quantam of Solace* lent the brief, five-minute segment plenty of star quality. For all that, she remains a mere apperitif next to Anne Parillaud's free-spirited Marie, the quirky and beguiling crème de la crème of French vamps.

Kiefer Sutherland as David in *The Lost Boys*

'Sleep all day. Party all night. Never grow old. Never die. It's fun to be a vampire.'

David's gang of bikers live an idyllic life of sorts in the sleepy Californian coastal resort of Santa Carla. A cool, devil-may-care posse of hot longhaired teenagers and twenty-somethings, they seem to do as they please on the town's streets and beaches, running wild while kicking the asses of any rival gang stupid enough to get in their way. To top it all, David's outlaw bikers appear immortal – they're even able to fly. It's the teen rebel dream of total freedom, liberated from rules and responsibility of any kind, with the edge of a blood-stained nightmare. By day, they must hide from the light, hanging like bats from the roof of a dark, dank cave. Even for the lost boys, immortality comes at a price – that of drinking human blood. Between them, David's little crew are responsible for making Santa Carla the murder capital of the world. They are, of course, vampires.

David – described by *Rolling Stone* magazine as 'the most raffishly charming vampire ever' – is played by Kiefer Sutherland. Of course, he's now internationally famous as Agent Jack Bauer, terrorist-busting hero of the hit TV series *24*, but it was *The Lost Boys* that first made Kiefer a pin-up, when the film debuted in 1987. 'His vamp gang leader flashed a style just attainable enough to inspire parent-upsetting trends,' observed *Entertainment Weekly*, who made him number fourteen in their '20 Greatest Vampire' list. (They compare his style to that of the post-punk rocker Billy Idol – a singer whose look has also been likened to that of Spike, *Buffy the Vampire Slayer*'s own undead rebel-turned-unlikely sex symbol.) The vampires of *The Lost Boys* take to their bikes in a mixture of vintage militaria, rocker jewellery and biker black leather, chests bared, long hair whipping in the wind as they hit the highway on their two-wheeled steeds. David's gang have been described as bikers, punks, followers of the post-punk New-Wave style of the '80s, or even MTV vampires.

However you choose to categorise them, *The Lost Boys* were surely the first Hollywood vampires to join the counterculture – the first undead who weren't just literally cold as the grave but street cool. (Anne Rice had her most famous vampire become a rock star in *The Vampire Lestat*, published two years previously, but the authoress's forays into

Kiefer Sutherland as David, the role that first made the star of 24 into a popular pin-up.

the contemporary music world are among her least convincing.) 'I don't know a single teenager who doesn't want to pretend or at least look like a rock star for a moment,' observes Kiefer of the wish-fulfilment aspects of his too-cool-for-school bloodsucker David. The film both feeds off and fed into youth culture in the '80s, swiftly becoming a hit on the college circuit, despite lukewarm reviews from mainstream critics. It was the film that not only launched a million teenage crushes with its cute young cast, but also established the link between the undead and alternative youth, with vampires who'd look more at home at a concert than in a crypt.

'Now you know what we are, now you know what you are. You'll never grow old, Michael, and you'll never die. But you must feed.'

'Cry Little Sister', the film's haunting theme song, is now a staple on many Goth dancefloors, while the angelic spectre of Jim Morrison (singer with the Doors) seems to loom over *The Lost Boys*. Morrison, the edgiest rock star of the psychedelic '60s, died in 1971, yet rumours persist that his death was faked. Such legends of immortality, combined with tales of the vocalist undergoing blood rites with occult confederates, suffuse the legacy of Jim Morrison with oddly vampiric overtones. The Doors' song 'People Are Strange' also features on *The Lost Boys*' soundtrack – as covered by Echo and the Bunnymen, a post-punk alternative rock band with a strong Goth following. The film had a substantial, if tricky to quantify, impact on youth culture. It certainly gave the burgeoning Goth movement a metaphorical shot in the arm, paving the way for leather-clad vampire aficionados, alongside those borrowing styles from the Victorian elegance of Hammer horror or the eighteenth-century chic of Anne Rice's *Vampire Chronicles*.

It's a tribute to the film's ability to transcend fickle teen fashion that David's undead gang still look as hip today as they did two decades back. *The Lost Boys* even gets away with the gravest hairdressing crime of the modern age, as its hell-raising bikers sport the same long-at-the-front, short-at-the-back style popular in the '80s, but since cast into fashion perdition as the much-mocked 'mullet'. 'It seems a bit wrong to pine for someone with a mullet – but we just do,' confesses Francesca Steele, who awards Kiefer's David a place in her recent 'Top 10 Sexiest Vampires' piece for the *Times*. Mullets notwithstanding, according to Sutherland himself, *The Lost Boys* is a film that retains its appeal 'from generation to generation. I have a 26-year-old stepdaughter and a sixteen-year-old daughter and both have found that film in their own time, and certainly not from me – they found it from their friends and things like that. I think that's phenomenal, that a film can get handed down from one generation to another and another, and do that, and that really is a testament to Joel.'

Kiefer attributes much of the film's success to its director Joel Schumacher, who had a hand in almost every aspect of the production, allowing him to be what Sutherland describes as 'explosive and expressive with the wardrobe elements and the set design', ensuring the movie's hip visuals matched Schumacher's original vision for *The Lost Boys*.

David's hip gang of biker bloodsuckers.

'Joel had such a fantastic sense of style that I remember knowing that this was going to be special,' says the actor. 'No film at that time had costumes like that, or had a look like that. You could just see it. You could see it from the sets, to the wardrobe, to the make-up, all the way down the line. I remember being just amazed to see from the original screenplay that I read, to watching the movie he was making – they were two completely different entities. That was when I began to realise the incredible power a director has.'

The director in turn pays tribute to Kiefer's part in making *The Lost Boys* a cult hit – and David such an iconic vampire. 'He can do almost anything, because he's a born character actor,' says Schumacher, 'and he was at eighteen, and you can see it in *Lost Boys* because he has the least amount of dialogue of anyone in the movie, but his presence is extraordinary. The minute he shows up on screen, you just go, "Vroom – who is this guy!?"' David has some stiff competition in the sex symbol stakes from his fellow vampires, Marko, Paul and Dwayne (played by Alex Winter, Brooke McCarter and Billy

Sleep all day. Party all night. Never grow old. Never die.
It's fun to be a vampire.

THE LOST BOYS

WARNER BROS. PRESENTS A RICHARD DONNER PRODUCTION A JOEL SCHUMACHER FILM
"THE LOST BOYS" COREY FELDMAN JAMI GERTZ COREY HAIM EDWARD HERRMANN
BARNARD HUGHES JASON PATRIC KIEFER SUTHERLAND AND DIANNE WIEST
MUSIC BY THOMAS NEWMAN EDITED BY ROBERT BROWN DIRECTOR OF PHOTOGRAPHY MICHAEL CHAPMAN
EXECUTIVE PRODUCER RICHARD DONNER STORY BY JANICE FISCHER & JAMES JEREMIAS
PRODUCED BY HARVEY BERNHARD DIRECTED BY JOEL SCHUMACHER
SCREENPLAY BY JANICE FISCHER & JAMES JEREMIAS AND JEFFREY BOAM

Wirth respectively) – all of whom have pin-up potential. Completing David's undead gang are the kid Laddie (Chance Michael Corbitt), and the glamorous Star (Jami Gertz), the female vamp who serves to reluctantly tempt the film's hero, Michael, into becoming their nocturnal collective's latest recruit. Michael is played by Jason Patric, a heartthrob in his own right, but there is no doubt that it is Kiefer's bestubbled bad boy David who steals the show.

'My character happened to have the really cool lines at the end of a scene,' says Kiefer. 'He'd have the one great line, so I'm deeply grateful to Joel for those.' Like fellow fanged blonde Lestat, David is a wholly unrepentant vampire, more inclined to joke at the expense of his victims than to dwell on the moral implications of his curse. He clearly relishes tormenting Michael during his hair-raising initiation into the gang, tricking him into believing that he's eating maggots, luring his unsuspecting recruit into ever greater acts of suicidal bravado by sardonically challenging Michael's youthful machismo. Sutherland's David is the ultimate bad boy no good girl could take home to her parents, but yearns to tame. Hip and irresponsible, David's the undead ancestor of Hollywood teen rebels like James Dean in *Rebel Without a Cause* or Marlon Brando in *The Wild One* – all punk attitude and biker swagger with catwalk-model looks.

'How are those maggots? ... Maggots, Michael. You're eating maggots. How do they taste?'

Of course, David will always be in a class of his own, distinguished from other big-screen teen mavericks by a simple fact: he was a vampire. The man entrusted with finding a look for the undead villains of *The Lost Boys* that made them frightening without compromising their sex appeal was effects artist and self-confessed 'monster geek' Greg Cannom. 'Joel was very specific about what he wanted,' he recalls. 'He wanted a very sleek aerodynamic look to them, but he was also using all of these young actors, who were really young model-looking, good-looking kids, so he didn't want to make them look like monsters, but he wanted something.' Greg's solution involved focusing on the vampires'

Some have noted a resemblance between David and the post-punk rocker Billy Idol,
(who has also been compared with Spike).

The Lost Boys kick some ass.

eyes, employing eerie contact lenses – then an innovative technique – and fashioning facial prosthetics that could give the bloodsuckers a more grotesque appearance without obscuring their faces.

In the end, the inspiration behind David's make-up came from an old photo of Cannom's. Intrigued, he noted how the high contrast emphasised this portrait of a tennis player to sinister effect. So, could the same principles be applied to his leading vamp? Cannom revealed: 'Kiefer, to age him a bit – because he was so young-looking – he had a beard, so I had to work around the beard [...] So I did these little cheekbone pieces and then I did the forehead piece that did the evil look coming down to the nose. It was a very stylised, simple look, but I really wanted them to look young and sexy, even though it was a very demon, evil look. By moving their forehead and face they could really contort it to make it look evil, or they could still look good.' In *The Lost Boys*, the vamps' full make-up is only unveiled when bloodlust overtakes. This narrative strategy had been employed before in both *Blacula* and *Vamp*, films that use a grotesque facial transformation to indicate when the undead shift into predatory mode. But perhaps the best-known example of this comes from *Buffy the Vampire Slayer*. One glance at the bloodsucking prosthetics in this hit '90s TV series and it's difficult to imagine the effects team having never watched *The Lost Boys* before coming up with a concept of their own.

The Lost Boys also gifted Whedon's media-savvy series with the term 'vamp-out' – a reflection that the film shared with the series, not just a focus on youth culture, but heavy comedy overtones. In common with many other stars who'd rather not have a horror movie on their CV – in a genre still considered disreputable by many critics – Kiefer prefers to think of the film as a thriller. '*The Lost Boys* was a smidgen of a lot of stuff,' he says, 'from comedy to pop culture and on purpose – that's exactly what Joel wanted to do with it, with scary moments in it.' '*The Lost Boys* had an unknown cast and when I was shooting it the studio kept saying, "Joel, are you making a horror film or a comedy because the two won't go together!"' says Schumacher himself. In point of fact, *The Lost Boys* was part of a trend in '80s Hollywood for comedy-horror crossbreeds, a number of which were vampire movies like *Vamp* and *Fright Night*. When they work well together, laughs and chills can compliment each other beautifully, but in *The Lost Boys*, fans remain divided over whether the comic elements dilute or make the movie.

The most obvious example is the Frog Brothers, a duo of absurdly grave teenage comic-book clerks offering to use the knowledge they've garnered from horror comics to combat Santa Carla's vampire problem. They are perhaps a hangover from the original script, substantially reworked by Schumacher as one of his preconditions for working on the project. The film's title is taken from *Peter Pan*, the original 'Lost Boys' being a gang of children who refuse to grow up. In the original script – as in J.M. Barrie's classic play – the protagonists were all substantially younger. It was Schumacher's idea to administer a heady shot of hormones, ageing the leads and transforming *The Lost Boys* from a story about pubescent bloodsuckers into the hip tale of teen rebellion and coming-of-age that became such a substantial cult phenomenon.

'*The Lost Boys* was kitschy and fun,' reflects Kiefer. 'I think we both knew that [it] was going to be a fun ride and we were both cool with that.' 'Most of my films were dark horses, and I still like to take risks, I feel very comfortable with it,' reflects Joel Schumacher of his career, which continues to sail a course between commercial success and cult credibility. Despite the huge success of *24*, Kiefer Sutherland still insists that *The Lost Boys* retains a special place on his CV, just as the character of David retains an immortal place in many hearts – beating or otherwise. 'I think the vampire genre is a wonderful genre,' he said recently, when quizzed about Stephenie Meyer's *Twilight Saga*, the most recent undead fan phenomenon. 'I haven't had a chance to see it yet, although I did see some commercials where people are flying through the air and I thought, "Yeah, I remember doing that,"' he adds with a chuckle. 'I hope they had as much fun making *Twilight* as we did with *Lost Boys*. That had a huge impression on my life.'

Vamp

Grace Jones as Katrina in Vamp

'The first kiss could be your last.'

adies and gentlemen, I give you... Katrina!' intones the master of ceremonies at the sleazy After Dark Club, as its clientele of lost souls stare transfixed at the stage. This is no ordinary strip club... or, indeed, any ordinary MC – he likes to snack on cockroaches between acts. But After Dark's main attraction soon puts everything else out of the audience's minds. An ivory-faced, snarling vision in red, Katrina prowls the stage on all fours, pawing sensuously at her crimson cocktail dress with clawed black gloves to reveal a hard, sinuous torso, striped with tribal markings, clad in what looks like a cross between lingerie and medieval armour. Played by the inimitable actress, singer and model Grace Jones as part-geisha, part-big cat, part-Zulu warrior maiden, Katrina is one exotic dancer After Dark's dumbstruck patrons are unlikely to forget. Always assuming they survive the night, of course.

Strippers can certainly be sexy – it is, after all, pretty much the job description. They can also be sad, losing not just clothes, but dignity, to rooms full of horny losers... and then they can be *scary*. Feminist clichés aside, a lady able to reduce men to drooling idiots simply by dancing: who really has the power in a strip club? Such establishments occupy a dark place, often bordering not just the criminal underworld, but also a metaphorical sexual underworld of loneliness and frustrated desire – a place where lust becomes a commodity, or even a weapon. The perfect place then, for a nest of vampires? Certainly writer and director Richard Wenk thought so, choosing to set his 1986 horror-comedy *Vamp* in an illicit Los Angeles strip joint. The road accident that befalls our hapless heroes before they reach the club suggests, however, that the After Dark Club is only nominally in California.

As their car spins out of control, camera angles (and some dodgy effects work) suggest the trio have crossed a boundary between reality and an ominously exotic twilight zone where anything is possible. It's an impression highlighted by Wenk's tendency to light his film in lurid shades of red and green. *Vamp* is every inch a product of its era, complete with big hair, padded shoulders and jacket sleeves rolled up to the elbow. The '80s were

Grace Jones as the predatory stripper, Katrina.

a golden age for horror-comedies, and *Vamp* blends its undead chills with chuckles – chiefly courtesy of its heroes, college students trying to get into a frat house. Frat house and high-school flicks were also a feature of the decade, and *Vamp* owes at least as much to smutty adolescent comedies like *Porky's* as it does to *Dracula*. *Vamp*'s teen heroes – a duo of smug college boys, Keith (played by Chris Makepeace) and AJ (Robert Rusler) – soon begin to grate, to the point where you're tempted to root for the vampires.

Vamp would probably have disappeared among the plethora of lightweight teen-friendly horror flicks made in this era, had Richard Wenk not managed to cast '80s icon Grace Jones as the film's show-stopping head bloodsucker Katrina. It was a time when the iconic Jamaican-born model and singer was reaching the peak of her career. Playing a vampire stripper in a teen comedy may not have seemed the obvious career choice for a diva with the world at her feet. But unpredictability and eccentricity are Grace Jones's trademarks, bringing not just style and class, but a heavy dose of capricious chaos to everything she touches – including the volatile vampire queen Katrina. Bizarrely, the singer has no lines in *Vamp* (the quotes in this profile are taken from 'Seduction Surrender', a song of Jones's that features in the film), but still manages to dominate proceedings with her fearsome physical presence.

'Hard is the flesh, soft is the night.'

Grace's slender, elegant physique has seen her compared to a black panther, though her sinuous power and predatory poise is perhaps even more suggestive of a cheetah – particularly in the strip scene, which introduces Katrina to both the After Dark Club's mesmerised patrons and the film's audience – a strange, feline routine that is at least as sinister as it is sexy. When the audience of horny strip-club regulars are stunned into silence, it's a reaction shared by most of *Vamp*'s viewers. There can be little doubt as to who holds the power here… and it isn't the lonely men laying down their dollars to watch the dance. The bizarre costume worn by Grace for the dance contributes to her unnerving image – wire 'armour' underwear, tribal body paint, topped by a white face and crimson kabuki wig. The visual artist Keith Haring originally designed the outfit for Jones for her 1985 tour, intending to challenge ideas of race, gender and sexuality. In the context of *Vamp*, it comes across as both sexually provocative and more than a little kinky, encapsulating Katrina's paradoxically sensual yet steely-cold aura of stylish menace.

That menace is fully realised in the scene where AJ heads backstage to try to secure Katrina's services for a forthcoming party. The slick frat boy finally loses his cool when it becomes obvious that Katrina is more interested in his body than his money, and he thinks he's in for a little kinky action from the enigmatic dancer. The oily AJ gets a good deal more than he bargained for. Katrina quickly takes control. Bestriding her hapless quarry, she licks him like a leopardess playing with her food, before tipping back her head and sinking her fangs into her terrified victim. It's to *Vamp*'s credit that when she feeds, Katrina truly becomes a monster – her eyes roll back, her toenails extend like talons, and her face contorts around a mouth overflowing with bestial fangs. This is no

Above left: Keith (Chris Makepeace) gets menaced by a denizen of the After Dark club.
Above right: A trio of vamps work some '80s style (right) in Vamp.

demure vampire maiden nibbling prissily at a swooning victim's neck, but a horrific creature chewing noisily on a screaming throat.

It fits entirely with Grace Jones's unique, animalistic appeal, and adds a welcome nasty edge to the film, which is in frequent danger of becoming a little too tame and cheesy. The DVD release features some fascinating extra footage of Grace rehearsing the scene. AJ has not been cast at that point, so Richard Wenk fills in for Robert Rusler as Katrina's unwitting supper. Even without any of the make-up or special effects, Grace's performance is unnerving to say the least. At once both wonderfully weird and terrifyingly tactile, the giggly relish with which she hungrily nuzzles Wenk is a little too convincing for comfort. Wenk does well to keep his composure as his lead actress toys with his throat.

Grace Jones has displayed a prodigious talent for keeping the international media enthralled with her unpredictable antics, while serving as a muse for a succession of leading artists and photographers. She transcended her original role as a disco diva in the '70s to embrace a New Wave sound in the '80s, with classic club hits like 'Pull Up to the Bumper' and 'Slave to the Rhythm' that helped define the decade. It was her striking image that really became iconic in the era, however, as she experimented with a range of bold, arresting looks to emphasise the androgynous qualities of her tall and highly toned, slender physique. It was this Amazonian quality that led to Grace being offered several film roles in addition to *Vamp*, typically in exotic dominatrix-style parts.

HAS JAMES BOND FINALLY
MET HIS MATCH?

ALBERT R. BROCCOLI Presents

ROGER MOORE

as IAN FLEMING'S

JAMES BOND 007

A VIEW TO A KILL

Starring TANYA ROBERTS · GRACE JONES · PATRICK MACNEE and CHRISTOPHER WALKEN
Music by JOHN BARRY Production Designer PETER LAMONT Associate Producer TOM PEVSNER
Produced by ALBERT R. BROCCOLI and MICHAEL G. WILSON Directed by JOHN GLEN
Screenplay by RICHARD MAIBAUM and MICHAEL G. WILSON Title Song Performed by DURAN DURAN

ORIGINAL MOTION PICTURE SOUNDTRACK
ON CAPITOL RECORDS AND CASSETTES

'Cries fill the dark.
I feel your embrace.'

In the sword and sorcery 1984 blockbuster *Conan the Destroyer*, she plays the fierce spear-wielding warrior Zula, opposite Arnold Schwarzenegger in the title role. Asked for advice on how to get a man by the film's heroine, Zula responds, 'Grab him! And take him!' The muscle-bound Schwarzenegger is reported to have complained that Grace was 'too tough' during filming. The following year she took the role of May Day in the James Bond film *A View to a Kill*. May Day is the lead villain's steroid-pumped girlfriend, until she discovers his plan to betray her and joins forces with Bond, played by Roger Moore. Moore, who has a reputation as a practical joker on-set, got a taste of Grace's own wild sense of humour during the scene where he seduces her.

'Roger has the hardest legs of any man I have ever felt,' she later recalled. 'He also had this gag he would do just before his love scenes. He would always have some kind of contraption under the covers and when you got under them he would goose you with it. I heard about this, and my great friend [now Bond film producer] Barbara Broccoli, who was in charge of looking after me during filming, and I agreed: "Let's get him first, before he gets me." So, we went to props and we got this very big black sex toy and we put white spots on it to make it look diseased. When I came back on the set and I had to take my robe off, I had it strapped on and I jumped on him. Roger roared with laughter. But Roger was great, you know. He showed me what he had for me: it was like a six-pronged carrot!'

That same disconcerting unpredictability and alarming physicality has characterised her infamous off-stage antics – most notably an encounter on a BBC chat show in 1981. When Grace felt that the host, Russell Harty, was ignoring her, she subjected the stunned Harty to a salvo of slaps – an episode voted 'the most shocking TV chat show moment' in a 2006 poll. She's recently staged a comeback, reflecting candidly in interviews over her past career, as well as the tendency to intimidate interviewers and audiences which helped her secure her part in *Vamp*. 'You know sometimes when you are sort of scary to some people it's their concept,' she insists. 'Because I'm not scary – the people that really know me know that I'm not scary. I pretend very good scary. I can be very good scary.

'I think it's probably because of the way I was brought up actually. Because, you know, I was brought up in a very, very strict way. I was brought up in a scary way. And maybe that's probably why my personality has this scariness… I think I'm just pretty straightforward and I think a lot of my audiences kind of enjoy being scared. You know, I watch scary movies, at a certain point I enjoy being scared. I think we all kind of enjoy that – there's a certain masochism – you know, with that and – but life is – life is also like that, as well you know. And I think one has to kind of […] I confronted it, like you say in a therapeutic way and it is a part of me, you know? So I do use it theatrically, I use it. I think it's the fact that I do that makes it more special actually.'

Whatever the reason, there's no denying that Grace Jones is as inimitable as she is intimidating – an authentic original – and she couldn't help but create one of the most memorable bloodsuckers to ever grace the silver screen. There are comparable performances, however. In 2002, another black diva, the R&B singer Aaliyah, took the title role in an adaptation of Anne Rice's *Queen of the Damned*. Aaliyah plays Akasha, another vampire queen with roots in Ancient Egypt. (*Vamp* hints that Katrina may once have been a queen of the Nile by having her sleep in an Ancient Egyptian sarcophagus.) The film was a modest success, though critics were less than enthusiastic, with some cynics even speculating that Aaliyah's tragic death shortly after the film's completion helped bolster the reputation of an otherwise lacklustre effort.

There have been a number of undead strippers over the years, most notably Salma Hayek's sizzling turn as Santanico Pandemonium in *From Dusk Till Dawn* in 1996. The serpentine Santanico is certainly as sexy as Katrina – worthy of a profile in these pages – and *From Dusk Till Dawn* is arguably a better movie than *Vamp*. But Salma's performance doesn't quite pack the raw animal charge Grace Jones brings to the screen. Katrina is inhuman to the point of being bestial – a grotesque predator made all the more deadly by her intense sexual magnetism. While *Vamp* is unmistakably a slice of '80s camp, Grace Jones's performance transcends any cultural context to achieve a kind of timeless fascination – alluring, appalling, even alien – but also strangely authentic and truly unique.

Dracula

Frank Langella as Count Dracula in *Dracula*

'Throughout history he has filled the hearts of men with terror and the hearts of women with desire.'

Inside a lonely abbey, cobwebs cascade down grandiose stone staircases like symphonies in decay, while outside the wind howls across the moors, lashing the majestic cliffs with pitiless rain. At the heart of this cobwebbed kingdom sits – not a spider – but a dark and dapper gentleman of impeccable charm. Yet he is every bit as deadly as any arachnid. In the 1979 production of *Dracula*, distinguished stage actor Frank Langella played the Count as a romantic and witty conversationalist – a man in need of no supernatural powers to supplement his natural charisma. He wasn't exactly new to the role, having had two years' experience playing the part in an award-winning stage production. It was the most successful theatrical *Dracula* ever staged. 'The crowds outside the stage door were uncontrollable and certainly the closest I have ever come to knowing what it would be like to be a rock star,' revealed Frank himself.

The *New York Times* described Langella's Dracula as 'a stunning figure […] tall, pale, Byronic, with an occasional prosaic reflex, as if he were mentally counting coffins'. The film version aimed to capitalise on the enormous success Frank had enjoyed as the Count on stage, amplifying his achievement with a hefty budget and lofty production values. Exteriors were shot on location in Cornwall. Doubling for Whitby, the area boasts some of the most breathtaking scenery the British coastline has to offer. Producers hired an eminent supporting cast, including Laurence Olivier, the most illustrious actor of his generation, as the Count's nemesis Van Helsing. The services of the legendary film composer John Williams were also secured to provide the soundtrack. Yet upon release, this *Dracula* apparently sank without trace, seldom even figuring in many modern memories of the myth, the same performance which once entranced theatregoers, scarcely figuring as a footnote in the Count's cinematic history.

So what went wrong? The stake through the heart of the 1979 *Dracula* might be summed up with the simple phrase, 'disco Dracula'. This version of the vampire Count fell victim to cheese rather than sunlight. Something about Langella's performance is evocative of the very worst of the '70s: the decade that taste forgot. Happily there is

Frank Langella – 'Disco Dracula' or one of the most underrated Counts in cinema history?

no disco music in the film – though Dracula's courtship of Lucy does feature a laser lightshow that almost begs a boogie beat. (Vampire films that do feature disco music – such as *Dracula Blows His Cool* – are generally worth avoiding.) But Frank's bouffant hair and white silk shirt, unbuttoned to reveal a supernaturally hairy chest, suggest he'd be as happy strutting his stuff in *Saturday Night Fever* as rising from a Transylvanian crypt. Yet fashions change – as yesterday's style taboo becomes tomorrow's hip look – and the '70s have slowly come back in from the cold, bringing Frank Langella's *Dracula* with them, the film gradually becoming a slow-burn success in the fledgling video rental market.

Most importantly perhaps, the 1979 *Dracula* deserves a re-evaluation because, overall, it's actually rather good. Not least Langella's performance as the vampire Count, which is both original and magnetic. He is among the most human versions of the Prince of Darkness – Frank refused to wear fangs for the role ('nobody is frightened by fangs', reasoned the actor) – employing native charm as his principal weapon. If some of his costumes are a bit too evocative of the sex symbol clichés of the era in which the film was made, it's worth remembering that he's not the first or last to tailor his image to contemporary tastes.

While Bela Lugosi's legendary portrayal of Dracula looks archaic to our eyes, the black dinner jacket and white shirt topped by slicked-back hair were pretty much the uniform of the fading matinée idol when the Lugosi version was made back in 1931. Hammer's cult horror films of the 1960s and '70s may have been set in the 1800s, but the female vamps and victims they featured wore low-cut gowns, boasting coiffures that owed as much to the fashion of the era in which they were made as their Victorian settings. In short, perhaps we should cut disco Dracula a little slack in the style department.

You will be flesh of my flesh, blood of my blood.
You will cross land and sea to do my bidding. I need your blood.'

'Langella makes Dracula sexy, fascinating, and therefore dangerous,' according to the film's director, John Badham. 'Evil doesn't have to be repulsive. I don't mind saying he's the only American actor in years who can play with style, who can wear capes, who can carry it off. It's tough to get away with that sort of thing.' (It evidently never occurred to Badham that the cape would be the least of the Count's problems in the fashion department.) The secret of Langella's characterisation success was the careful consideration he brought to the part, crafted over a lengthy period of preparation for playing the Count on stage. 'What I had to find was a key to what would make him work today,' Frank explained. 'I decided he was a highly vulnerable and erotic man – not cool and detached and with no sense of humour and humanity. I didn't want him to appear stilted, stentorian or authoritarian as he was so often presented. I wanted to show a man who was evil, but lonely and who could fall in love.'

The result was the most romantic interpretation of the role to date, not to be challenged until Gary Oldman donned the cloak some thirteen years later in *Bram Stoker's Dracula*.

Dracula with his willing victim, Lucy (played by Kate Nelligan) – the roles of Lucy and Mina are effectively reversed in this version.

With some critics it proved an instant hit. 'What an elegantly seen Dracula this is. All shadows and blood and vapours and Frank Langella stalking through with the grace of a cat,' applauded Roger Ebert. 'The film is a triumph of performance, art direction and mood over materials that can lend themselves so easily to self-satire.' But the *New York Times'* critic captured the general feeling better. 'In making this latest trip to the screen in living color, *Dracula* has lost some blood,' she observed. 'The movie version [...] is by no means lacking in stylishness; if anything, it's got style to spare. But so many of its sequences are at fever pitch, and the mood varies so drastically from episode to episode, that the pace becomes pointless, even taxing, after a while.'

'It was an enormously difficult role for me to play,' Langella later confessed. 'I didn't begin to grasp Dracula until I was close to opening in the play in Boston for the previews. Then I finally began to understand him through his *humour*.' Some critics have blamed the failure of Langella's popular Dracula to transfer from stage to screen on a change in emphasis. The play allowed for far more camp, while Badham's film is by and large

Whilst overall a very romantic version of the story, the Langella Dracula *does contain some effective moments of horror, such as when Mina (Jan Francis) rises from the grave.*

a deadly serious affair. For others, the film is simply a little anaemic. By making him sympathetic, Langella drains Dracula of some of his menace, while the supporting cast – good on paper – are a little stiff in action. Laurence Olivier in particular makes for a feeble Van Helsing – proof if such were needed that horror, while looked down upon by 'proper' actors, is one of the most challenging genres to work in.

There are however, some highly effective scenes. Certainly, the one played out in the catacombs beneath Whitby churchyard, in which Van Helsing comes face to face with his daughter, Mina, freshly risen from the grave, is the stuff of authentic nightmare. In fact, John Badham's *Dracula* is a terminally uneven film, suffering from the same dichotomy that would provoke criticism of Francis Ford Coppola's adaptation years later. Horror fans complained of an excess of romance, while viewers of sentiment were turned off by the lashings of crimson horror. Yet, for those willing to simply let the overblown storytelling and lush Gothic visuals wash over them, both films make for highly satisfying cinematic experiences, buoyed by powerful performances from their respective leads. Both Frank Langella and Gary Oldman manage to convey the contradictory nature of their respective Counts as essentially noble, passionate figures imprisoned within the arcane confines of a supernatural curse.

Time is on my side. In a century, when you are dust,
I shall wake and call Lucy, my queen, from her grave.

To fully appreciate Frank Langella's interpretation, you almost certainly had to catch it in the theatrical production. The actor later recalled that he received unorthodox appreciation from couples who watched the play, husbands assuring him the day after seeing his Dracula, 'Boy, did my wife make love to me that night!' So how did Frank realise such an erotically-charged creature of the night? 'One day in rehearsal I couldn't get the first act, when Dracula enters and is introduced to Van Helsing and the other characters,' he later recalled. 'I suddenly thought to myself, how would I feel if I'd been lying in a box all day and, when I got up, there was an invitation to dinner with two pretty girls, the doctor who lived next door and a young lawyer? I would be rather delighted because I had something to do, and also because it would be fun to toy with these mere mortals. When that sense of pleasure in what he was came to me, other things began to develop and he became a man who seduced his victims rather than attacked them.'

'I also came to the conclusion that there was an aspect of the Count that had never been fully explored before – his vulnerability, his sensitivity, his fear,' added Langella. 'I've always felt that he's the kind of man, if he has lived for 500 years and experienced different times and different cultures and different peoples, who's bound to have gained a certain amount of philosophy about life, so that he doesn't spend all of his time lurking and looking for blood. He needs blood to survive, but when he gets it, he has another ten or twelve waking hours to pass. He can enjoy the company of other people, he can find himself more attracted to one woman than another – it doesn't have to be purely indiscriminate bloodletting.'

Many films become cult favourites by virtue of being low-budget, low-profile productions that slip under the critical radar upon release, only to be recognised as neglected classics in retrospect. Nineteen-seventy-nine's *Dracula*, however, is a more unusual case: a big-budget movie that seemingly sank without trace, but has been gradually rediscovered by a new generation of audiences. Like all cult movies, it's far from perfect – the pace flags, and Langella's immortal Count still seems a little stuck in the '70s – but the overall package will enchant all true devotees of Gothic romance. Since then Frank Langella's career has quietly flourished, with some now hailing him as one of the finest American actors of his generation. An award-winning performance as the disgraced US President Richard Nixon in *Frost/Nixon* – another role that transferred from stage to screen – has attracted particular praise from film critics.

Perhaps he was lucky that his Count wasn't a runaway Hollywood sensation. Actors like Bela Lugosi and Christopher Lee made an indelible impression as Dracula, but struggled to be taken seriously in any future role. Meanwhile, Frank Langella still has warm memories of his tenure as the Prince of Darkness. 'Whether he came across sexy or not wasn't on my mind,' he recalled in a recent interview with CBS News to promote *Frost/Nixon*. 'But then I grew to understand when women fainted, and when they were carried out of the theatre, I thought, "Oh, I'm onto something here."' 'Women literally fainted?' gasped the interviewer. 'Yeah, they did,' replied Langella. And how did that make him feel? 'Oh, I loved it!' he laughed.

Blood for Dracula

Udo Kier as Count Dracula in *Blood for Dracula*

'He'll go right to your neck and you'll go right to his heart.'

Many cinematic depictions of Dracula have captured at least some of the pathos of his character – the eternal loneliness and tragedy behind the seductive charm and unearthly horror of his curse. Few, however, have gone so far as to portray the Count as truly pathetic. Yet this assumption lies at the core of Udo Kier's unforgettable performance in the 1974 cult flick *Blood for Dracula*. The last of his dwindling bloodline, his is perhaps the only Count you could actually pity. In the opening credits, we witness the malnourished Dracula applying black dye to his greying hair and eyebrows, and rouge to his lips, in a feeble attempt to maintain appearances. Similarly, while other vampire films have chosen to depict his lust for blood as an addiction, few Dracula flicks have taken this interpretation to its logical conclusion, with the hapless Prince of Darkness as much a slave to his hunger for blood as any junkie undergoing involuntary cold turkey. The enfeebled Count is even rendered wheelchair-bound for part of the film.

It's a tribute to Udo's ineffable oddball charisma and contagious enthusiasm that, despite all this, there is something endearing and sympathetic, even sexy, about his down-at-heel Dracula. 'My biggest fans are from vampire films,' laughs the impish veteran actor. 'I get fan letters from women wearing leather bikinis in a dungeon with a whip. They love it.' With his sharp, old-world dress sense and effete manner, he's the quintessential decadent, a simpering aristocrat rendered all but impotent by his unnatural lifestyle. Painfully pale and thin, with his slicked-back bottle-black hair, delicate, almost effeminate features, and tendency towards self-pity and wild over-excitement, he's certainly one of cinema's most memorable Counts. Kier's Dracula wastes more time bickering with his long-suffering, equally inept and excitable secretary Anton (played by Arno Juerging) than he does actually seeking out victims.

These comedy elements add further to the unique mood and unorthodox style of *Blood for Dracula* and the saving grace of its whining Count is that he's not only handsome in his own darkly elfin fashion, but also very funny, courtesy of Kier's mercilessly camp performance. It's a kind of hardcore *Rocky Horror Picture Show* – revelling in the same

Udo Kier as Andy Warhol's loveably pathetic Count Dracula.

sick brand of comedy that leaves one half of the cinema's patrons rolling in the aisles, while the other storm out feeling nauseous. Particularly gut-wrenching are the numerous indignities suffered by Kier's Count – from sending Anton with a sponge to the scene of a car accident to licking corpuscles from the floor in a situation that doesn't bear repetition in polite company – in order to obtain virgin blood or, more precisely, 'wergen blood!' The German actor's heavily-accented pronunciation of the word, 'virgin', is just one of an array of madcap in-jokes that invariably bring the house down among cult audiences at midnight screenings, though the instances when accidentally ingested non-virgin plasma causes Dracula to violently vomit crimson cascades into the nearest toilet bowl might challenge even the most hardened fans of black comedy.

'Paul Morrissey wanted me to vomit eight litres of blood out of my body, which I couldn't take, in *Dracula*,' Udo recalled recently, naming this as the most outrageous director's request of his career. Nonetheless, it was *Blood for Dracula*, and its preceding companion piece *Flesh for Frankenstein* that first brought the actor to international attention. Sometimes billed as *Andy Warhol's Frankenstein* and *Andy Warhol's Dracula*, both were produced by the world-famous US pop-art svengali to capitalise on his reputation in the art world, though the real vision behind the two films was director Paul Morrissey. 'I prefer *Dracula* to *Frankenstein*,' reveals Kier, when pressed to choose his favourite. 'Because *Frankenstein* was in 3D and to shoot a film in 1973 in 3D, it was very time consuming, and you couldn't have any close-ups, because you looked like Pinocchio when they did a close up. So, it should have been Frankenstein meets Pinocchio. I also like *Dracula* better because it was more poetic – that would be the film if I had to choose one.'

'I have no coffin to sleep in; the kitchen is full with impure meat. We've been travelling for days … No progress!'

Blood for Dracula came together in a fairly haphazard fashion when *Flesh for Frankenstein* wrapped sooner than anticipated. Indeed, languishing between roles was never an option for Udo. 'I had just finished *Frankenstein*, and I was very sad,' laments Kier. 'So on my last day I went to the cantina and had a bottle of white wine. Paul Morrissey came in and said, "Well, it looks like we have a German Dracula."' I said, "Who?" He said, "You. But you have to lose ten pounds over the weekend." So, I didn't eat anymore and just had water. That's why in *Dracula* I had to sit in a wheelchair. I had no more power. I was sweating all over because I had to wear that fur coat, and it was so heavy and I was so weak that I could hardly walk… Yes, I was crawling all the time. Paul said, "Oh, that's good. Crawl up the stairs." You know how sadistic directors are. "Did it hurt you? Yes? Good." But it was fun, and it started everything off, because Andy Warhol was very big then. All of a sudden I was in *Vogue* magazine. All of a sudden I was bumped up to first class, and you know how that is. You become like a little baby.'

An ad hoc, improvised style and air of chaos characterises the film, lending it much of its bizarre charm. The multinational, multilingual cast often appear barely able to understand each other while, according to Kier, there was frequent improvisation on set.

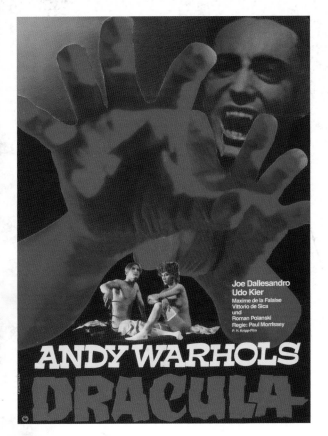

Joe Dallesandro
Udo Kier
Maxime de la Falaise
Vittorio de Sica
und
Roman Polanski
Regie: Paul Morrissey
P. H. Kniµ-Film

ANDY WARHOLS
DRACULA

'*Dracula* was interesting because we started shooting but we didn't know how to end it!' he says. 'So we improvised. I told [the director] I liked cooking, I liked herbs and Paul said, "Oh good! Do a scene where you go into the kitchen and say you want herbs, but you don't want *garlic*!" So that's how it all came along.' The plot concerns the Count's attempts to secure a fresh supply of virgin blood, which has run dry in his native Transylvania. (While few vampire films make much of the tradition that the Count can only drink virgin blood, *Blood for Dracula* uses the idea as a comic comment on how rare virginity has become in today's liberal society.)

So, the ailing Count heads reluctantly to Italy – faithful servant Anton in tow – on the basis that such a Catholic country must be overflowing with virgins. Dracula settles upon a bankrupt Italian nobleman's daughters as his potential victims. Unfortunately, the Marchese's beefcake gardener, played by the American actor Joe Dallesandro with his thick Brooklyn accent, has already had his wicked way with all of the girls bar the youngest in a series of explicit sex scenes. Now he has his lustful sights set on the last virgin in the family. 'I'd love to rape the shit out of her,' explains the less-than-sensitive stud, in a line calculated to ensure *Blood for Dracula* further tests the boundaries of good taste. Giving the art-house crowd something to sink their teeth into, the gardener's also a committed Communist, haranguing the hapless Dracula with tirades on how the aristocracy are finished, destined to be overthrown by the working classes.

In the circumstances, it's easy to sympathise with Udo's hapless Count, particularly when he meets his grisly, pathetic end, in a scene which owes as much to *Monty Python* as splatter cinema. 'When I did *Dracula*, it was very funny and very poetic in a way,' reminisced the actor. 'This poor Dracula, he wouldn't do any harm to anybody, but he had to get the blood of a virgin just to live. So he goes to Italy because he hears they're religious, but they're all whores, and he gets more and more sick. So, you see, there's a poem behind it. Francis Ford Coppola's *Dracula* was such a mixture of Fellini … of course, Gary Oldman is one of the best actors, but they tried to make Dracula erotic and

The Count finds a victim – sadly not a 'wergen'.

for me the movie wasn't. In Polanski's film, he shows it as a comedy, which was much more erotic because it wasn't pretentious.'

'The blood of these whores is killing me.'

The film Udo's referring to is 1967's *Dance of the Vampires*. Like *Blood for Dracula*, it's a vampire spoof with strong art-house appeal, this time courtesy of its Polish director, Roman Polanski – then regarded as the most promising young director of his generation among film connoisseurs. *Dance of the Vampires* is Polanski's tribute to the classic horror films made by Britain's Hammer studios, though with production values most Hammer directors could only have dreamt of. Beautifully shot with stunning snowbound sets, in many ways it outdoes its inspiration in creating a haunting, bleak winter wonderland, with some wonderful set-pieces, such as the undead ball of the film's title. Let down by weak humour which never quite gels with the film's powerful ambience of evil and decay, *Dance of the Vampires* might have been a masterpiece of Gothic cinema if played straight. Polanski claims the film was ruined when Hollywood producers re-cut it for US release. Hoping to make it more 'kooky and cartoon-y', they retiled the film *The Fearless Vampire Killers, or Pardon Me, But Your Teeth Are in My Neck*.

The 'eroticism' alluded to by Udo comes courtesy of the film's leading lady, Polanski's fiancée and the stunning Hollywood sex kitten Sharon Tate. Sharon plays the role of Sarah, an innkeeper's daughter who's captured the affections of both head vampire

Count von Krolock (brilliantly played by Ferdy Mayne) and incompetent young vampire-hunter Alfred (played by Polanski himself). It's easy to see why they're both captivated – Sarah is the essence of wide-eyed sensuality, the ravishing redhead apparently innocent to the electrifying effect she has on every red-blooded male around her, the *New York Times* praising her 'chillingly beautiful but expressionless performance'. Her previous innocence makes the final scene even more of a heart-stopping jolt and if Sarah had spent more time undead, Sharon Tate would probably have qualified for an entry of her own in this volume. Tragically, *Dance of the Vampires* was one of Sharon's final films – in 1969 she was brutally murdered in the infamous Manson Family massacre.

Comedy and vampires go way back – as long as bloodsuckers have provided popular entertainment, there have been attempts to satirise them. Even the Parisian fad for vampire plays in the early 1800s was swiftly followed by a number of stage parodies. Bela Lugosi first popularised vampires on the big screen with his legendary portrayal of Dracula in 1931. Yet the decline of his career was signalled by a series of self-parodying roles in mockery of his own most celebrated performance, beginning with the Count in *Abbot and Costello Meet Frankenstein* in 1948. Subsequent to *Dance of the Vampires* and *Blood for Dracula*, Hollywood made a number of notable Dracula parodies. In 1979, veteran matinée idol George Hamilton made a credible comedy Count in *Love at First Bite* – 'Your favorite pain in the neck is about to bite your funny bone!' promised the film's tagline – while in 1995, actor Leslie Nielsen and director Mel Brooks confirmed the undying popularity of *Bram Stoker's Dracula* with their spoof version, *Dracula: Dead and Loving It.*

However, nobody has quite topped the over-the-top, bad-taste battiness of *Blood for Dracula* – nor Udo Kier's inimitable performance as Hollywood's most lovably neurotic Count. The indomitable Udo has gone on to a prolific career, mostly in villainous roles. 'Personally I like to cook, garden and plant trees,' he confesses with a disarming grin. 'But when I put a tuxedo on I am evil.' To date, the German actor has well over 150 films to his credit – both as a formidable force in cult cinema, and a familiar face in mainstream Hollywood, alongside roles in countless commercials and even rock videos for artists as diverse as Madonna and Korn. He remains best known, however, as a horror icon, both donning the fangs and falling victim to the vampire's kiss in movies like *Shadow of the Vampire* and *Blade*. 'My favourite scene in *Blade* is the club scene in the beginning when they are dancing and the blood sprays down all over them,' laughs Udo. 'I think blood looks very good on the breasts of women. It's so erotic. When do you have the chance to massage bloody breasts? Never!'

William Marshall as Prince Mamuwalde in *Blacula*

Blacula! – Dracula's Soul Brother!' exclaimed the publicity for this oft-neglected cult classic. It obviously worked, as the trailer became a big draw in its own right; some inner-city cinemas apparently even delayed the release of the film itself to avoid losing the crowds that came to enjoy the trailer. *Blacula* was released in 1972, in the golden age of 'blaxploitation' – one of a wave of low-budget, sensationalist movies made with black casts, aimed at black audiences. Most were violent thrillers like *Sweet Sweetback's Baadasssss Song* and *Shaft* (both released in 1971), featuring plenteous ass-kicking action and hip soul/funk soundtracks. Yet *Blacula* stands out in more ways than one. A fully-fledged horror, *Blacula's* also a film of sufficient quality to break out of its cinematic ghetto, enjoying crossover success beyond regular blaxploitation audiences. Sure, it has the pumping funk and sweet soul sounds you might expect, together with the afros, roll-neck jumpers and other groovy styles that make such films priceless fashion time capsules for connoisseurs of camp.

But contrary to the impression given by much of its promotion and the movie's memorable, but brash title, *Blacula* is more than a kitsch oddity in which a jive-talking, polyester Prince of Darkness struts his stuff to vintage Motown. Indeed, fans of the cheesy content of much classic blaxploitation are often disappointed by the lack of cheap laughs to be had here. Beneath its garish, funk-laden façade, *Blacula* is a serious vampire film with a few genuine chills. 'We were shooting a street scene in Los Angeles one night, when a very beautiful woman wearing a long black cape approached me,' recalls its star, William Marshall. 'She introduced herself and then startled me by saying that she wanted to be a vampire! "Why?" was all I could weakly think of replying, my mind mostly on the scene I was about to play. Her eyes lit up at this. "Because vampires live forever!" she exclaimed. "There's really no way to kill them. If you pull the stake out of their hearts, they revive. They can't really be hurt, no matter what happens." I turned away from her not knowing what to say. But I've never really forgotten her words.'

William Marshall as blaxploitation's own Dracula, Prince Mamuwalde.

The lion's share of the credit for the unique character and success of *Blacula* belongs to William Marshall, who imbues its titular vampire with charm, menace and – most importantly – dignity, courtesy of his evident wit and intelligence. An imposing six-foot-five-inches tall, the handsome Indiana-born actor not only lends weight to his role, but also insisted on modifying the script to give him something to truly get his teeth into. The film's villain was originally called plain old Andrew Brown, but the plot was amended to include a prologue that gave his character both motivation and a name to conjure with. 'I suggested an African hero who had never been subjected to slavery,' William explained, 'an African prince travelling to Europe with his beloved wife, to persuade his "brother" European aristocrats to oppose the African slave trade.

'*Blacula* is the first classic vampire film to be written for black central characters,' elaborates the actor. 'The premise of the story is provocative and the characterisation of the central figure – in the writing of which I was invited to participate – is unusual and interesting. An African spokesman, Prince Mamuwalde arrives in Europe in 1815 [in the final script, the date is changed to 1780] with his bride, on a mission of protest against the renewal of the slave trade following the invention of the cotton gin. The prince's tour of Europe brings him to the Balkans, and one night he and his wife attend a dinner at the castle of Count Dracula. That's when all the problems begin...' The contemptuous Count – a sneering racist – infects his guest with vampirism and seals him in a coffin, separating the African prince from his beloved wife, Luva. While Mamuwalde is tortured by his newborn craving for blood, he is tormented by the terrible sounds of his bride starving to death.

'Sir, I suddenly find your cognac as distasteful as your manner.'

THE BLACK PRINCE OF SHADOWS
STALKS THE EARTH AGAIN!

SAMUEL Z ARKOFF PRESENTS

SCREAM
BLACULA
SCREAM

AN AMERICAN INTERNATIONAL PICTURE RELEASE STARRING
WILLIAM MARSHALL · DON MITCHELL · PAM GRIER
Michael Conrad · Bernie Hamilton INTRODUCING RICHARD LAWSON Color BY MOVIELAB
EXECUTIVE PRODUCER SAMUEL Z. ARKOFF SCREENPLAY BY JOAN TORRES & RAYMOND KOENIG AND MAURICE JULES
STORY BY JOAN TORRES & RAYMOND KOENIG PRODUCED BY JOSEPH T. NAAR DIRECTED BY BOB KELLJAN

BLOODSUCKER!
Deadlier than Dracula!

Warm young bodies
will feed his hunger
and hot, fresh blood
his awful thirst!

"BLACULA" IS
THE MOST
HORRIFYING
FILM OF
THE DECADE."

BLACULA

"BLACULA" STARRING WILLIAM MARSHALL · DENISE NICHOLAS · VONETTA McGEE
GORDON PINSENT AND THALMUS RASULALA CO-STARRING EMILY · LANCE · CHARLES
YANCY · TAYLOR, Sr. AND MACAULEY COLOR

Fast-forward to the twentieth century, and two gay interior designers buy the contents of the deceased Dracula's Castle to ship back to Los Angeles, unaware that their purchase includes the sealed coffin of the undead African prince. 'Where we come from, Dracula is the crème de la crème of camp,' crows one, anticipating a huge profit from their Transylvanian bargain hunt. (While *Blacula* may satisfy opponents of racism, others have accused it of laying the homophobia on rather thick.) Of course, it's not long before an undead Prince Mamuwalde is let loose on the streets of '70s LA, thirsting for blood. His bloodlust is tempered, however, when he encounters a girl named Tina who is the spitting image of Luva. Tina's sister's boyfriend happens to be a black police scientist named Dr Gordon Thomas, who begins to suspect that there's a vampire at large, and the stage is set for a showdown between Blacula and the LAPD.

The reincarnation of a lost love has become a cliché of horror cinema (the same plot lies at the heart of *Bram Stoker's Dracula*), but *Blacula* moves along at such pace that it doesn't seem tired here. In particular, once again, William Marshall's performance makes all the difference. Even though Tina is sceptical of this curious stranger's insistence that she is his bride of centuries past, Mamuwalde's mannered seduction makes her surrender to his charms wholly plausible. His deep dulcet tones, old-world charm, leonine good looks and powerful presence are enough to make any maiden weak at the knees. Marshall's flashes of ferocious rage are equally impressive. Whether surrendering to Blacula's aching bloodlust or lashing out at anyone foolish enough to stand between him and his

Blacula sinks his teeth into the reincarnation of his lost love (played here by Vonetta McGee).

cherished, newly discovered bride, Mamuwalde's ancient fury unleashed makes for some truly compelling viewing. Only Blacula's passion for his lost love is stronger than the curse that makes him thirst for human blood, making the African Prince as tragic and sympathetic as he is threatening.

In fact, William Marshall was in possession of an impressive acting CV even before he took on the cape of Blacula, with parts in a wide range of TV serials, such as *Star Trek* and *Bonanza*, and films as diverse as *Demetrius and the Gladiators* and *The Boston Strangler*. Like a number of cinematic vampires, William had a background treading the boards in serious drama. (John Carradine, for example, was a noted Shakespearean character actor before he became one of Hollywood's less celebrated Draculas in the 1940s.) His most acclaimed performance was in the title role of Shakespearean tragedy *Othello*, which toured the theatres of Europe. The *London Sunday Times* hailed Marshall as 'the best Othello of our time'. While cultured critics might sneer at the suggestion, there are parallels between the characters of Othello and Prince Mamuwalde. Both are tragic, noble black anti-heroes, driven to violence by outrageous circumstance, and it is to Marshall's credit that he appears to have approached both parts with equal seriousness.

He believed in researching his roles (one account suggests that fifteen years went into his preparation for the part of the celebrated abolitionist Frederick Douglass) and *Blacula* was no exception. 'I knew very little about vampires before I became involved in this project,' confessed William. 'So I took a crash course in Dracula, reading the book and looking at some of the earlier films. I also talked to people about *why* audiences are still so responsive to the story after all these years. Perhaps most important of all as an actor, I had to know about vampires from the vampire's point of view. And not just any vampire: how would an African prince of the early nineteenth century feel about being taken captive in

William Marshall's performance combined menace with true pathos.

Transylvania and doomed to live out eternity hungering for human blood? What I learned I put into the film. And perhaps the most interesting thing I discovered was that an effective vampire movie must be flooded with urgent emotions of anguish, yearning, terror and, ultimately, relief.'

Marshall's suggestion of weaving slavery into the background of *Blacula* added an intriguing dimension to his character as well as the story. It also spotlighted one aspect of the vampire myth seldom explored in horror cinema. In effect, the anti-slavery campaigner Prince Mamuwalde himself becomes a slave to his bloodlust after Dracula bites him. He in turn enslaves others with his bite. Unlike Mamuwalde, himself, the vampires he creates appear feral and devoid of their former personalities – more akin to ravening zombies than the debonair bloodsucker of Hollywood myth. The question is often posed that, given the chance to live forever, enjoying supernatural powers, why is vampirism considered such a curse? The answer in part lies in the concept of slavery. Is immortality – tantamount to enslavement to bloodlust – really such a boon if its price is your free will?

'Our people are renowned as hunters. Almost two centuries ago the ruling elders of my people sent me and my bride to Europe on a mission to protest the slave trade. On that mission I myself was enslaved, my wife murdered and I was placed under the curse of the undead. Our assassin was a vampire. Count Dracula.'

On the subject of zombies, it is interesting to note that, previous to their Hollywood reinvention as post-mortem cannibals, this species of living dead were principally those condemned to labour beyond the grave as slaves by black magic. The legend has its roots in Haiti, a Caribbean nation born of a slave rebellion raging around the same time that the prologue for *Blacula* is set. The film that changed the popular image of zombies from undead slave labour to flesh-eating ghouls was the low-budget, 1968 classic *Night of the Living Dead*. Interestingly, a number of horror movie scholars in the '70s regarded the film as a radical new spin on the vampire genre, destined to change the face of vampire cinema, rather than spawn a whole new sub-genre of horror cinema (the word 'zombie' is never used in the film). Coincidentally, the black actor Duane Jones plays Ben, hero of *Night of the Living Dead* – the first time an Afro-American was cast as a non-ethnic lead in a major movie, suggesting that horror audiences are commendably colour-blind.

Duane Jones's next film role was in *Ganja & Hess*, a 1973 blaxploitation vampire movie launched in the wake of *Blacula*'s success. It proved too slow-moving and subtle for mainstream audiences, and the horror theme put off most high-brow critics, but this strange saga of an ancient Nigerian blood cult is highly rated among modern connoisseurs of offbeat cinema. The same year, Mamuwalde was back in *Scream, Blacula, Scream* (a title which William Marshall hated), though opinion is still split on whether the film was a pale imitation of its predecessor, or a credible companion. It did at least feature Pam Grier, queen of blaxploitation, as the voodoo priestess with whom Mamuwalde falls in love. (Grier took the title role in *Jackie Brown*, Quentin Tarantino's 1997 homage to blaxploitation.) Subsequent black vampires have proven a mixed bag. The 1974 comedy *Vampira* is almost certainly best forgotten, the brittle British romantic lead David Niven plays an ageing Count Dracula, horrified when his lost love reincarnates as a jive-talking black woman. In 1986, *Vamp* presented a formidable female vampire in the form of the Jamaican-born singer and model Grace Jones.

The popular Afro-American comedian Eddie Murphy takes the lead in the 1995 comedy *Vampire in Brooklyn* as the suave bloodsucker Maximillian. The film has its fans, though this author is not among them. At the same time independent film studios were courting black audiences, comic book companies began launching black superheroes in response to more enlightened attitudes. Among them was Blade, an indomitable vampire-hunter, who was himself half-vampire and debuted in 1973, in the comic *Tomb of Dracula*. Blade finally made it onto the big screen in 1998, played by the actor and martial artist Wesley Snipes. In contrast to his loquacious comic-book incarnation, the cinematic Blade is a taciturn killing machine. The film was popular enough to spawn two further films and a TV series, becoming Snipes's most successful role, though whether he qualifies as a classic vampire, rather than just another generic action hero with a gimmick, is open to question.

Surely few vampire aficionados could deny that William Marshall's acting abilities easily eclipse the limited range of Wesley Snipes, or that Mamuwalde's magnetic menace makes Blade's macho posturing look crude and adolescent by comparison. To say that William Marshall is the undisputed king of the black vampires is missing the point. His performance in *Blacula* – a cheap flick lesser actors would have taken as an excuse to sleepwalk – places Marshall among Hollywood's undead aristocracy by any measure. The actor himself has never resented that he became better known for a blaxploitation horror movie than his acclaimed Shakespearean roles. 'I daresay the vast majority of people don't go to the theatre, so I don't mind that I'm still so strongly identified with *Blacula*,' he said. 'Early on, young black people who didn't know my name would yell at me on the street, "Mamuwalde… hey, Mamuwalde!" It was especially pleasing that I was being called by the African name I gave the character. I asked one young fan, "Who do you think I am?" He said, quoting from the nightclub scene, "You know, you're the strange dude!"'

Daughters of Darkness

Delphine Seyrig as Countess Elizabeth Bathory in *Daughters of Darkness*

'An erotic nightmare of vampire lust.'

Imagine if you will, an attractive young couple on honeymoon, travelling across Europe. Headed for England, they find themselves in Ostend as winter descends. The Belgian port is a bleak destination out of season, which somehow mirrors the cracks already beginning to appear in the relationship between Stefan and his new bride Valerie, as they check into a grand, deserted cliff-top hotel. Bound by powerful physical passion, both have secrets that throw shadows over their fledgling union. They are not alone for long, as two glamorous new guests arrive – an impossibly chic Hungarian Countess, and her secretary, a coquettish brunette with her own boyish charms named Ilona. The quartet of guests soon become acquainted in the empty hotel, the young couple beguiled by the old-fashioned charms of the beautiful Countess, who introduces herself as Elizabeth Bathory.

But the hotel concierge is haunted by a recollection of the Countess visiting back when he was still a bellboy. She doesn't appear to have aged a day in 40 years. Meanwhile Stefan becomes embroiled in a heated discussion about the bloody atrocities perpetrated by Elizabeth's sixteenth-century namesake, 'the Crimson Countess', who Elizabeth claims to be an ancestor of hers. To Valerie's growing unease, the conversation builds to an almost pornographic intensity, as Elizabeth drapes herself around Stefan's shoulders, goading him into increasingly explicit descriptions of the Crimson Countess's crimes. Delphine Seyrig's performance as Countess Bathory is one of the most powerfully erotic and chillingly stylish in the history of vampire cinema. Released in 1971, *Daughters of Darkness* isn't a conventional horror film by any means. A Belgian art-house flick that focuses on sexual fascination and emotional violence rather than gore or Gothic thrills, it remains one of the most visually seductive explorations of erotic bloodlust in cult cinema, a beautifully shot, feverish dream of a film in which the characters are drawn into an increasingly heady vortex of dark sexual tension.

At the centre of this hypnotic dance of death is Delphine, the cold, art-deco decadence of her surroundings chiming perfectly with her depiction of a modish femme fatale, whose impeccably elegant smile conceals a chill sadistic streak. The film's French title,

Delphine Seyrig as Elizabeth Bathory – equal parts Marlene Dietrich and Countess Dracula.

Les Lèvres Rouges, translates as 'the red lips'. When we first see the Countess, she is all in black, her crimson lipstick the only facial feature that shows clearly through her funereal veil of lace. She changes her costume numerous times throughout the film – from a slinky figure-hugging red number to a metallic reptilian gown – but those crimson lips remain a constant, set off by matching fingernails that resemble nothing so much as elegant talons. According to the film's director, Harry Kümel, 'We had arranged so many fancy clothes and dresses for Delphine Seyrig that we had hardly any money left to get the other actors decent clothes!' Her image evokes the lost glamour of forgotten Hollywood stars of the 1920s and '30s. The Countess, with her elaborately styled platinum coiffure, brings to mind the iconic blonde German actress Marlene Dietrich. While her travelling companion Ilona is strongly reminiscent of the American starlet Louise Brooks, with the dark bobbed hair and smouldering eyes to match.

'I have seen many a night fall away into an even more endless night.'

Very little is explicitly stated in *Daughters of Darkness* – there are no fangs or obvious supernatural elements – the Countess preys upon the young couple using her sophisticated charm and manipulative personality. Yet, the film's ambiguity invites the viewer to speculate. What if Stefan's stories of the original Countess Bathory are true? What if consuming human blood really did keep the infamous sixteenth-century sadist young forever? What might she look like? How might she behave? By the twentieth century the traditional aristocracy were in decline, so might she not have taken on the appearance and manners of their successors – Hollywood's new aristocracy of screen gods and goddesses? We never know for sure whether Delphine's character Elizabeth is the original Countess, kept young by her bloodlust, but Harry Kümel cleverly evokes the exquisitely macabre erotic undertones of one of history's most infamous and disturbing cases of serial murder.

The real Countess Elizabeth Báthory was born in 1560, a member of one of the most distinguished dynasties in Hungary, with extensive lands in Transylvania. In 1610 she was convicted of a range of appalling atrocities and walled up in her own castle, where she died four years later. (Some scholars now believe she was innocent, framed by rival nobles anxious to confiscate her lands, though the balance of historical opinion still says she was guilty.) The crimes had a strong lesbian, sadistic psychosexual character. Her principal victims were serving girls, who she beat, burned, stabbed and tortured in a variety of brutally imaginative ways. Some were covered in water, then left to freeze to death, naked in the castle courtyard. Estimates as to how many died as a consequence of Báthory's bloodlust vary. In the scene where she discusses her 'ancestor' with Stefan in *Daughters of Darkness*, Delphine's Countess observes that some say as many as 800 died, adding 'a woman will do anything to stay young'.

'She believed human blood was the elixir of youth,' explains Stefan to his horrified young bride. 'I've read of her. She kidnapped young girls and kept them chained, to give blood, blood for her to bathe in and drink. And she hung them up by the wrists and

Above: Unsuspecting couple Stefan (John Karlen) and Valerie (Danielle Ouimet) find themselves drawn further into the Countess's web. Below: The Countess and her secretary Ilona (Andrea Rau) conspire.

whipped them until their tortured flesh was torn to shreds.' 'Oh yes, that's it, and she clipped off their fingers with shears,' breathes the Countess, with evident excitement. 'And she pricked their bodies with needles,' adds Stefan. 'Yes, she tore out their nipples with silver pincers,' sighs the Countess, to Valerie's increasing distress. 'She bit them everywhere, and then she pushed white-hot pokers into their faces and when they parted their lips to scream, she shoved the flaming rod up into their mouths,' enthuses Stefan. 'She pierced their veins with rusty nails and slit their throats.' 'Until their white bodies pumped their young blood over her naked skin,' interrupts the Countess, apparently entering an orgasmic reverie. 'Blood, beautiful red blood, over her hands and her arms and her legs and her face…'

Rumours abounded after her conviction of the sadistic sexual and occult motives behind Countess Báthory's crimes, though actual trial transcripts always remained under lock and key and her very name became taboo in polite Hungarian society. Tales of her bloodlust and occult quest for eternal youth combined with her tendency to bite her victims, her title and her Transylvanian homeland, led some to speculate that it was Elizabeth Báthory who first inspired the author Bram Stoker to create the character of Dracula in his famous Victorian novel. 'Local people in the Cluj area still refer to Dracula as a woman,' said the Transylvanian-born academic Dr Zoltan Meder in a 1975 newspaper story on the subject. 'Possibly it was male chauvinism,' he added as to why the author might have changed the sex of his lead character. 'Stoker may have felt that the world would not accept such horror being attributed to a woman.'

'Love can be stronger than life. Stronger even than death.'

Issues of twisted sexuality and gender play a prominent part in *Daughters of Darkness*, contributing to the film's miasmic atmosphere of decadent perversity. It is implied that the Countess and Ilona are lovers – Ilona becoming jealous when her mistress takes an interest in the newlywed couple, and less than enthusiastic when the Countess instructs her to seduce Stefan. Countess Bathory's own interest in Stefan is clearly just a ruse to get closer to his young wife Valerie. Stefan is a less than sympathetic character, a dishonest sexual sadist with – it is implied – an older male lover waiting for him in England. Any 'message' in the film is left deliberately confused. Is it a celebration of female power, as personified by the immortal Countess Bathory, who clearly doesn't need any man? Or a demonisation of lesbianism as dangerous and deviant, as embodied by Delphine's parasitic femme fatale?

There have been numerous cinematic treatments of the life and crimes of the Crimson Countess, ranging from the hokey 1973 horror film, *Curse of the Devil*, in which the Countess is a vampire queen battling a heroic werewolf, to the historical 2008 film *Bathory*, portraying her as the innocent victim of a conspiracy. Among the more memorable are *Immoral Tales* (1974) and *Countess Dracula*, released the same year as *Daughters of Darkness*. *Immoral Tales* is a compendium of erotic tales by the cult Polish director Walerian Borowczyk. Elizabeth Báthory is the subject of the third story in the film, in which the statuesque Paloma Picasso (daughter of the famous artist Pablo) plays the Countess. In this sexually provocative vignette, she assembles a gaggle of nubile young girls to satisfy her cruel compulsions. *Countess Dracula* was made by Britain's famous Hammer studios as a vehicle for their new star Ingrid Pitt – however, we cover Ms Pitt's pulchritudinous Gothic charms in greater detail later in the book.

As far as many connoisseurs are concerned, *Daughters of Darkness* remains the definitive cinematic interpretation of the Countess Báthory story, as well as one of the most atmospheric and artful horror movies ever made. Harry Kümel spoke about achieving atmosphere, and its importance to the genre as a whole, in *Flesh and Blood Compendium*, telling his interviewer Mike Lebbing that 'the secret of horror movies is that they should be as realistic as possible. That's what I reproach Clive Barker for; he tells his stories in an unrealistic framework. Stephen King doesn't do that, even in his worst books the horror is placed in a realistic context. That's the strength of *Daughters of Darkness*... Of course that hotel is absurd because it hasn't got any personnel,' he laughs. 'But people don't see it because the context is realistic. It's at that moment that you have to give reality a push and then you get the effect of fear, inner fear... It's like what went wrong with Coppola's *Dracula*: he chose a style in which he tried to be too special. The thing is, you have to dare to be as realistic as possible... The weirder your subject is, the more normal you should film it. Then you'll get the proper effect.'

Kümel is dismissive of the script he put together for *Daughters of Darkness* with his two collaborators, Jean Ferry and Pierre Drouot. 'We wrote the story in three days,' he told Lebbing. 'Pierre Drouot and I thought that the only way to make our lousy story work was to cast one of the biggest actresses of that time. Now, Pierre had this big obsession: he wanted to get between the sheets with Delphine Seyrig,' laughed the director. 'Really, he had enormous fantasies about all the things he could do with her. But I thought that when I would meet her to talk about the script, she would kick me out of her house. When I arrived in Paris and met Delphine, she had already read it – she thought it was excellent and wanted to do it.'

Kümel, who has a habit of being dismissive of his own movies, is less than enthusiastic about Delphine's fellow cast members, insisting that the actor and actress who play Stefan and Valerie were imposed upon him by the film's producers. But he does allow that German actress Andrea Rau, who plays Ilona, 'had some charisma'. Kümel also concedes there was some real chemistry in the scenes she played opposite Delphine Seyrig's Countess: 'She loved the interaction with Andrea Rau very much. Delphine really has a talent for that, and she's also extremely intelligent... Delphine did a wonderful job. The only thing I had to do was to put her in the right frame.' Sadly, the Lebanese-born actress died in 1990, but *Daughters of Darkness* remains as a lasting tribute to her captivating beauty and sophisticated charm. 'With her flawless style and timeless beauty – who needs Botox when you've got the blood of 800 virgins?' concludes *Entertainment Weekly*, who rightly award Delphine Seyrig's Countess Bathory a place in their '20 Greatest Vampires'.

The Vampire Lovers

Ingrid Pitt as Carmilla Karnstein in *The Vampire Lovers*

'Even the dead can love.'

As the film that helped inspire the title of the book you're now holding in your hands, the 1970 Hammer horror flick *The Vampire Lovers* clearly holds a special place in the affections of this author. Few would argue it's the best movie listed in these pages and, among such distinguished company, only the most dedicated of Ingrid Pitt's many fans would claim she outshines the competition in the acting stakes. But as an example of a performance that captures the erotic appeal of the undead, Ingrid's Carmilla Karnstein sets a standard few can match, leaving an indelible impression on many young horror fans, this one included. Her character is at once innocent and calculating, both a classic vampire and a wholly individual interpretation of the archetype. The actress has become an undead icon, her image familiar from countless horror books and magazine articles.

Photographs of her as Carmilla in *The Vampire Lovers* and the sixteenth-century Hungarian aristocrat and bloodthirsty sadist Elizabeth Bathory in *Countess Dracula* are still routinely reproduced in such media. But it is the shot of Ms Pitt baring her fangs in the 1971 anthology movie *The House That Dripped Blood* – in which she gleefully parodies her own vampiric persona – that remains most iconic of all. Familiar to many unfamiliar with Ingid's work, this powerful image transcends the context of *The House*, providing ample evidence that she encapsulates the popular image of the seductive creature of the night. Equally ample and evident is Ingrid's impressive cleavage, laid bare by a low-cut gown. The fact that the actress wasn't shy of unveiling her voluptuous assets in her vampire roles undoubtedly influenced the decisions of some picture researchers when looking for a shot to add spice to their layout. But if Ingrid's appeal rested simply on her easygoing attitude to nudity and knockout figure – or indeed, her distinctive, Eastern-European beauty – she would be merely one among a plethora of actresses to turn heads in the history of horror.

Instead, Ingrid Pitt is widely acclaimed as the queen of horror, chiefly courtesy of the two films she made with Britain's legendary Hammer studios. Her relationship with the studio began at a point of crisis for both Hammer and the Polish-born actress. Hammer's

Ingrid Pitt as Carmilla, the undead Countess who preys on young ladies.

head honcho James Carreras was painfully aware that the studio's regular recipe of suggestive Gothic horror was becoming tired, particularly faced with increasingly explicit chillers from their US competitors. Meanwhile, after a high-profile supporting role in the war film *Where Eagles Dare*, work was running dry for Ingrid Pitt, so, after meeting Carreras at a film premiere, she began to lobby him for work. 'I worked so hard on Jimmy Carreras, trying to get work that he finally said, "What do you want, blood?" And I said, "Yes! Yes!"' she laughs. 'So, I got all that blood, garlic, fangs and crosses.'

The project he had in mind was an adaptation of the 1872 vampire novella *Carmilla* by Irish author Sheridan Le Fanu, in a part which, Carreras warned her, would involve some nudity. *Carmilla* had previously been filmed as *Vampyr* by the legendary Danish director Carl Dreyer, way back in 1932, though this lingering, eerily nightmarish early version bears little resemblance to the original tale. The French director Roger Vadim made a version entitled *Blood and Roses* in 1960, while there was a 1964 Italian adaptation entitled *Crypt of the Vampire*, starring Hammer stalwart Christopher Lee. Nonetheless this was fresh territory for the British studio in more than one respect. Not least because the script was the first to explicitly exploit the lesbian undertones of the original story, in which a young girl is befriended and then slowly drained by the mysterious, feline vampiress of the tale's title, against the backdrop of the Austrian district of Styria in the 1800s.

Glamour, in the form of pretty actresses in cleavage-revealing corsets or clinging, diaphanous nightgowns, had always been part of the unique appeal of Hammer horror. In *The Vampire Lovers*, however, the studio responded to loosening censorship by introducing a dose of overt nudity and lingering girl-on-girl clinches to their well-tested brew of Gothic titillation. '*Carmilla*'s great,' enthuses Ingrid. 'Sexy dresses and lots of sultry languorous looks. I did read the novel before I played the part. A fat lot of good that did me. I completely missed the idea that it was a take on lesbianism! It wasn't until I was asked to introduce the film at a festival at the National Film Theatre that it struck home. There was a big poster saying it was the seminal lesbian/vampire movie. I just thought it was about a couple of friends, bored out of their skulls during a hot summer in Styria. And one of them happened to be a vampire. I'm just an innocent, I guess!'

'Your dress is pretty, but it's for a country girl. In town, you must be more sophisticated. You must take everything off. Try it once...'

Innocent, perhaps, but uninhibited certainly, Ingrid had no problems with the nudity the part demanded – it even seems to have helped bring out the devil in her! In an interview with Vic Buckner of the Crime Time website, the actress recalls that, 'when Jimmy Carreras offered me the part in *The Vampire Lovers*, I really did my homework about the phenomenon. And in Le Fanu's story, *Carmilla*, there is this strong sexual element. I think the director, Roy Ward Baker, really made it work – although the producers were two lascivious little chaps. On the way to do my nude scene with Madeleine Smith, I

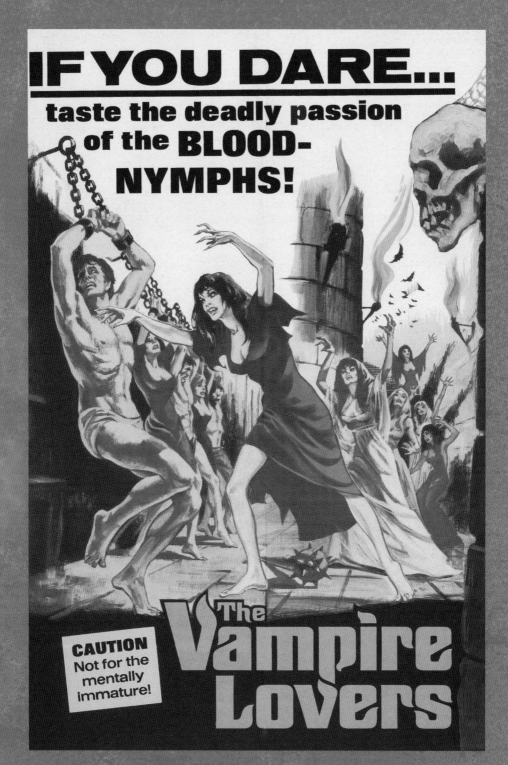

The Countess snacks on a slumbering peasant girl.

came out of the trailer with my dressing gown on and nothing underneath, and I saw these guys walking towards me with their heads down. I thought, what the hell, I'll make their day, and just flung open the dressing gown. Their reaction was priceless!'

Madeline Smith, who plays Carmilla's victim Emma, was another actress who achieved iconic status in Hammer horror films of the '70s. Though, in contrast to the predatory beauty of Ingrid, Madeline's image focused on her arresting doll-like pout and wide-eyed, girlish good looks. (In a disarmingly self-depreciating interview, Smith recently said, 'I knew how to pull gormless faces.') Madeline had worked for Hammer before, with a small part in *Taste the Blood of Dracula*, but the studio had concerns about her qualifications for her first starring role. 'I got a very worried phone call from the producer who said he was concerned about my lack of bosom,' she told the BBC in 2009. 'He said, "We like you a lot, but we don't think you are voluptuous enough." I reassured him, and then I scuttled off to Hornby and Clarke dairy round the corner and I bought every yoghurt I could find, and stuffed myself like you might fatten cattle, and it worked!' While such sentiments might not impress hard-line feminists, it's a refreshing contrast to the actresses who starve themselves into skeletal shapes (you might even argue that Hammer became an inadvertent champion of feminine curves, just as fashion was beginning to favour an unhealthily slender standard of feminine beauty).

Carmilla with her intended victim,
Emma (Madeline Smith).

On screen, Pitt's voluptuous Carmilla, with her husky Eastern-European accent, working her worldly-wise charms on Smith's redheaded ingénue makes for erotically-charged viewing. In keeping with their public personae, while Ms Pitt didn't bat a perfect eyelash at the more salacious scenes in *The Vampire Lovers*, Miss Smith had reservations. 'My nightie had to be pulled down to my waist and I had to run around with no top,' she recalls in *Hammer Glamour*. 'I wasn't exactly ecstatic about this, but when we were filming it one of the producers, Michael Style, told us that those scenes were for the Japanese version and that they wouldn't be seen over here. Of course, I later realised that there was no Japanese version, and that this was something he told us so he could get his way. I was a virgin when I made the film. I didn't know what a lesbian was and I had no idea what was supposed to be happening on that bed.'

Most modern viewers, witnessing the semi-clad horseplay that soon heats up into something steamier between Carmilla and her victim, might be sceptical, but these were more innocent times. To this day, Ingrid Pitt insists that her character's relationship with the naïve young Emma was not a lesbian one. 'If other people see it that way, that's fine. I didn't play it that way,' she explains. 'The whole film would have fallen flat on its face if I had believed that they were lesbians. The whole story hinged on the fact that Mircalla gave up her life compassionately for another being whom she loved. If there had been something sexual about it, it would have ruined this feeling of love that she had. And she truly loved Emma. It's a different feeling when you love somebody sexually. She gave her soul for this woman. It had nothing to do with the fact that she was a girl. If the creature had been a male, it would have been the same thing.'

There are interesting parallels here with the responses authoress Anne Rice and actor Tom Cruise gave to suggestions that the novel *Interview with the Vampire* and its subsequent cinematic adaptation were gay love stories. Issues of gender are a red herring by this argument. Like Lestat, Carmilla is neither male nor female, but a whole different species, thus making issues of heterosexuality or homosexuality irrelevant. Whatever you might make of such supernatural hair-splitting, there's no denying that Ingrid Pitt's performance breathes sexual hunger, though she nuances her Carmilla with

Hammer glamour – the female stars of The Vampire Lovers *pose for a publicity shot.*

an underlying sadness. She must drain those around her to survive, by the very nature of what she is, but some, like pretty young Emma, she slowly vampirises with something approaching tenderness, even love. (Peasant girls are treated more like convenient snacks.) We never quite sympathise with Carmilla, but when Hammer's veteran vampire-hunter Peter Cushing finally puts an end to her with one decapitating stroke of his sabre, we're left with ambivalent feelings indeed.

'I hate funerals, hate them! You must die. Everybody must die... Hold me!'

The Vampire Lovers proved a hit for Hammer, who swiftly went into production for two similar pictures, which later became known as the 'Karnstein Trilogy' (after Carmilla's family name). Despite a similar blend of bloodlust and heaving bosoms bared, *Lust for a Vampire* is generally regarded as something of a misfire. Part of the blame rests on production troubles behind the camera, with last-minute personnel changes and script rewrites necessitated by pressure from the censors. Part may also lie with the song 'Strange Love', played over the seduction scene in what must surely be one of the cheesiest musical interludes in vampire cinema. The true stake through the heart of *Lust for a*

Vampire, however, is its star. Replacing Ingrid Pitt as Carmilla Karnstein is the Danish actress Yutte Stensgaard. She's certainly got the looks – the shot of her sitting up in her tomb, her breasts dripping blood, remains iconic in the annals of erotic horror cinema – but once tasked with resurrecting Carmilla from the grave, the stunning Scandinavian blonde is painfully out of her depth.

Stensgaard's starring role came about as a result of Hammer's habit of spending as much time looking through modelling portfolios as acting resumes when searching for new female discoveries. A somewhat happier consequence of the practice came when Hammer executives came across Madeleine and Mary Collinson, featuring as the first ever twin Playmates of the Month in the October 1970 issue of *Playboy*. They cast the sisters as the leads in *Twins of Evil*, the final part in the Karnstein Trilogy. Maria (played by Mary) is virtuous, while her twin Frieda (played by Madeleine) is a wilful minx, swiftly seduced by the local vampire, Count Karnstein. *Twins of Evil* remains a firm favourite among Hammer fans, intoxicated by the heady Gothic cocktail of Satanism, witch-hunting and naked, nubile flesh. The Collinsons acquit themselves admirably, though neither can boast the presence or acting talent of Ingrid Pitt, and *Twins of Evil* was their last film together. By the end of the decade Hammer had also effectively ceased film production (though the studio looks set to finally rise from the grave at time of writing).

Hammer's Karnstein Trilogy looks very tame, even rather camp, to modern eyes, yet in its day comprised three groundbreaking films. 'I was the first female predator,' states Ingrid proudly. 'It's interesting that now most of those films are regarded affectionately, but they were criticised as beyond the pale in their day. Even the beheading in *The Vampire Lovers* was cut, and most TV prints don't have it.' In his entertainingly irreverent history of Hammer, *A Thing of Unspeakable Horror*, Sinclair McKay dedicates a chapter entitled 'Fangs are a Feminist Issue' to the studio's female stars. While he stops far short of suggesting that Hammer campaigned for women's liberation, he does point out that the horror studio gave far more powerful roles to women – both behind and in front of the camera – than their mainstream competitors. Asked recently by the BBC if she felt exploited, Madeline Smith responded dismissively that, 'I was a very willing exploitee – I didn't mind at all,' while Mary Collinson has described *Twins of Evil* as 'the best experience of our lives'. But, ultimately, was the connection between eroticism and the most feared predatory creatures of the night explored in such movies entirely healthy? 'Why not?' reasons Ingrid. 'Sexuality is a complicated thing, and films should reflect that.'

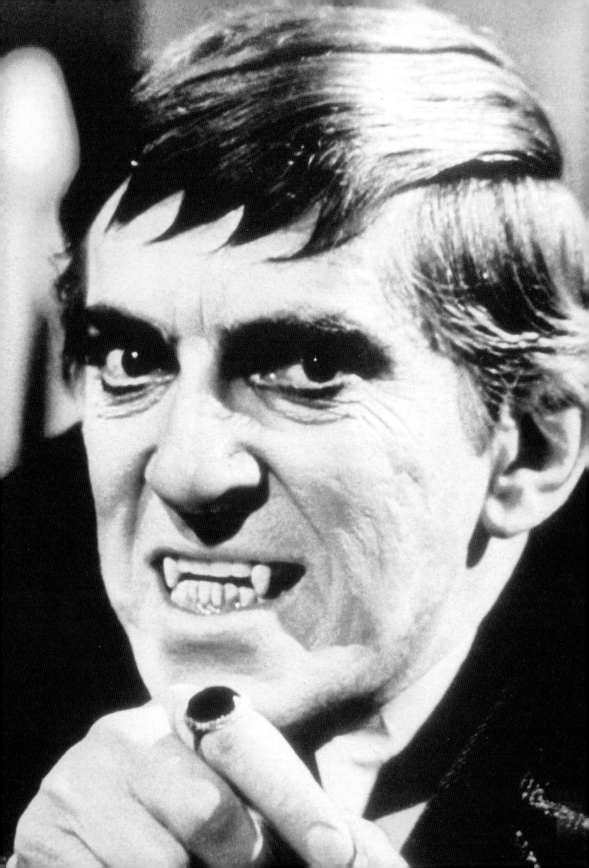

Dark Shadows

Jonathan Frid as Barnabas Collins in *Dark Shadows*

'A story of blood relations.'

For a whole generation of American youngsters, the highlight of every weekday was rushing home from school in time to settle down for the latest episode of the soap opera *Dark Shadows*. The credits open on the Gothic mansion of Collinwood, brooding atop Widow's Hill and overlooking the windswept Maine coast. Eerie music sets the scene for a show that owes at least as much to classic Hollywood horror as the standard soap format. Alongside the familiar plot devices of misunderstandings and domestic drama, passion and betrayal, the show features a cast of ghosts and golems, werewolves and witches. According to best-selling horror author Stephen King, in his folksy survey of the genre, *Danse Macabre*, *Dark Shadows* 'became a kind of supernatural mad hatters' tea party (it even came on the air at the traditional hour for tea – four in the afternoon), and hypnotised viewers were treated to a seriocomic panorama of hell – a weirdly evocative combination of Dante's ninth circle and Spike Jones'.

'One tuned into *Dark Shadows* every day, convinced that things could become no more lunatic,' adds the author. 'And yet somehow they did.' Stephen King was in his twenties when the series first broadcast between 1966 and '71 – a decade or so older than its core school-age audience. For them, the increasingly implausible plots and supernatural characters were no barrier to enjoying the show, younger viewers responding in particular to what contributor Pleasant Gehman describes in the Generation-X nostalgia bible *Retro Hell* as the soap's 'ultrasexy vampires'. A notable young fan was the pre-teen Johnny Depp, hooked by the show-stealing performance of *Dark Shadows*' star Jonathan Frid. Frid played the vampire Barnabas Collins, who Johnny later named as 'a huge obsession of mine. I loved Barnabas Collins more than I loved the Harlem Globetrotters. I wanted to be Barnabas Collins so much that I found a ring, it was probably one of my mother's rings, and I wore it on this finger, and I tried to comb my hair like Barnabas Collins, and I was trying to figure out how I could get fangs. It really had a heavy impact on me, a heavy influence on me.'

'The opening features spooky, unearthly music (I think it had a theremin on it, or

Jonathan Frid's role as Barnabas Collins made him an improbable pin-up among teenage fans.

at least that's what it sounded like) and a grainy film of waves crashing on a desolate, rocky beach,' reminisces Pleasant Gehman. 'There were all sorts of sexy, cleavage-heaving women fainting in tight-bodiced dresses, and lots of carnal love bites to the neck, flashing capes, people getting bricked up into walls, evil laughter, and always a cliff hanger on Fridays. *Tiger Beats* and other teen mags were full of the cast because they were so damn good-looking (Quentin [Collins, a werewolf] looked kind of like Adam Ant, if I recall correctly). The show came on from 4:00-4:30, so everyone would rush home from school, gather in the living room, pull down the shades so it was real dark, and get the shit scared out of them.'

While most of the *Dark Shadows* cast had their fans, none could rival the popularity of Jonathan Frid's Barnabas Collins. The screaming females who showed up at any personal appearance made by the actor became known as 'Frid girls', displaying symptoms of the same hysterical adulation usually reserved for pop stars. A somewhat bemused Frid later described himself as 'an ageing dreamboat to the bobby-sox generation of the time'.

In truth, Jonathan Frid does make for an unlikely teen sex symbol – a classically-trained stage actor, entering middle age when he took the part, with a broad face and a curiously serrated fringe, hardly fashionable either in the 1960s or the 1790s when Barnabas was first entombed. Only pronounced cheekbones, heavy eyeliner, a wolf's-head cane and a pair of fangs prevent the actor from resembling a somewhat avuncular accountant. It is a tribute to the timeless allure of the vampire that the role of Barnabas Collins transformed Jonathan Frid into a nationwide teen idol.

Jonathan himself has confessed to being totally taken aback by the popularity of his performance. 'I didn't actually have an audition, merely an interview,' he explained in 1968. 'Every time I go for a role, I'm always very aware of how I "look" to producers. However, I saw all these sinister-looking people who had come to read. I looked at one person and instantly thought he would get it – he looked marvellous. So I was interviewed and went home, never thinking another thing about it. A day later, I was called in again and that was it, I got the role! […] Meanwhile, I had planned to go west and get a teaching job, or do that along with some work in Hollywood, such as television or film… I thought the role on *Dark Shadows* would go on for about three or four weeks. And then, the phenomenon began, the role caught on, the mail started to flood in.'

Time is a rushing, howling wind that rages past me, withering me in a single, relentless blast, and then continues on. I've been sitting here passively, submissive to its rage, watching its work. Listen! Time, howling, withering!

At the height of the show's popularity, Jonathan Frid was getting 5,000 letters a week – many of them from love-struck female admirers. 'It gets rather exotic at times, I must say!' he smiled in a 1969 TV interview. Was any of it of a more worrying character, asked the interviewer? 'Some of it, but I think the majority of the mail is mail to an actor – I

As his character developed, Barnabas became an essentially tragic figure.

like to think of it as mail to an actor – who's doing a good job. We appreciate that there is mail of that kind. There is very little morbid mail really. Most of the mail that I find amusing is the kind of mail from people who really get involved in the story and they cannot imagine you as anybody else but the character you're playing. Even on tours I've been on, people come up to me and they really believe I'm a vampire. They really think I might bite them at any moment, and the letters are very much like that.'

But how to explain the mass of overexcited Frid girls outside the studio, waiting to catch a glimpse of their idol? When pressed, the actor responded that, 'I don't want to get into Freudian psychology – but I think the bite has a great deal to do with it. I also think that this guy Barnabas is a guy with a hang-up. Maybe people sympathise with the fact that he's got something to fight. I've really never been able to figure it out, but I'm enjoying it immensely.' Some critics have dubbed Barnabas Collins the screen's first reluctant vampire, while others have credited him as the first supernatural sex symbol. As readers of this book can attest, neither assessment is true, though he clearly had a profound impact on those young Americans for whom Barnabas was their first vampire, so to speak.

With the dubious exception of the vampiric characters who appeared in sit-coms, *The Addams Family* and *The Munsters* (both shows debuted in 1964), however, Barnabas was surely television's first undead soap star. The *Dark Shadows* format, as a serial screening five new half-hour episodes a week, had a large part to play in not only the character and popularity of the show, but also that of its lead vampire. Soaps have highly demanding schedules. There's little time for rehearsal or reading lines, while second takes are a rare luxury. Flimsy sets and threadbare production values are compensated for with the format's immediacy and intimacy. Regular viewers get to know the characters as old friends or even surrogate family members, and so it was with Jonathan Frid's interpretation of Barnabas Collins, who needed to hit the ground running, thrust into the series' 210th episode (1967) at a time when flagging ratings meant *Dark Shadows* was already under threat of cancellation.

Soaps typically cast parts to type, as actors have little time to prepare for their roles. In Frid's case, it resulted in the actor's unfamiliarity with television, translating effectively into the vampire's difficulty in coming to terms with modern America. 'I was uptight for the first year, and the interesting thing was, so was Barnabas,' he said in 1969. 'The two things worked very well together. Barnabas caught himself in the twentieth century – he was let out of a coffin and he had to adjust to all these things, so I, Jonathan Frid, had to adjust to a relatively new medium for me. So, if I ever goofed in a scene, I let Barnabas goof too if you know what I mean, and the two things worked very well. Now that Barnabas is fairly used to the twentieth century, so I have got used to the medium of television, and I find it very exciting doing a new show every day, I really enjoy it.'

Playing Barnabas Collins as uneasy, even awkward, was a true innovation in vampiric terms – a direct contradiction to the classic creature of the night, who's as self-assured as they are mysterious. 'I've made Barnabas go in a direction – I've humanised him,' said the actor. 'I don't think I'm a strict vampire as Bela Lugosi was. Bela Lugosi played strictly a vampire, he really was spooky – I guess I've been spooky at times, but I tend to play the man with a hang-up. He [Lugosi] played strict vampire – he was rather passionless.' While the familiarity of appearing five times a week diminished Barnabas Collins's mystique, it made him infinitely more approachable and sympathetic – somebody viewers like Pleasant Gehman could envisage inviting into her room on a moonlit night; a role model Johnny Depp could imagine growing into.

'At last darkness has come. Goodbye, Maggie Evans. I might have loved you, I might have spared you, but now you must die.'

Barnabas was always a flawed anti-hero at best – capable of ruthless villainy as well as moments of compassion – a victim of his own selfishness and weakness as much as his vampiric curse. Frid has observed that the essence of the character lay in 'the lies he told to himself' – something we can all identify with to a certain extent. 'In real life, I find that monsters are people,' observed the actor. 'We are all monsters to one another at some time or other. You catch a friend not telling the truth, or you are suddenly suspicious of them, you all of a sudden see a new glow in their faces – a new look. Now that's what I call a monster. Anyway, my face, my voice reflected my emotions of nervousness and tension; I could have done anything at that moment. I think that this is what established the character that first day.

'The key [to playing Barnabas] is telling lies with such finesse that the other characters in the story can't see through them... but of course the audience can,' observed Frid. 'They are in on everything. Be sure to keep the two groups apart.' This plot device – of a crucial secret that the characters miss much to the frustration of the viewer – remains a regular standby in soap operas today – supernatural or otherwise. It's been used in subsequent vampire serials, from *Buffy* to *Being Human* to *True Blood*, and Barnabas's immediate successors as undead pin-ups can be found among the stars of these shows. None, however, can compete with the sheer longevity of Jonathan Frid's deceptive, edgy bloodsucker. *Dark Shadows* ran for an amazing 1,225 episodes, before finally running out of steam and ideas in 1971.

It lives on beyond the grave in constant syndication and fan conventions, where devotees can meet its stars, swap memorabilia and recreate favourite scenes. Attempts were made to resuscitate the show by its original creator, Dan Curtis. Two films were made – *House of Dark Shadows* and *Night of Dark Shadows* – featuring gore and production values impossible on the small screen. But, lacking the intimacy of the series and the presence of Barnabas (Frid's name is missing from the cast of *Night of Shadows*), both movies failed to match the success of the original serial. In 1991, Curtis attempted to revive the series in an updated version, with actor Ben Cross as Barnabas. Yet despite also featuring horror icon Barbara Steele, and a positive reception from fans, this latest incarnation was cancelled after just a dozen episodes. Some blamed scheduling clashes with extensive news coverage of the Gulf War, though it was largely a victim of the more cutthroat attitude of modern networks, who frequently cancel shows before they've even had a chance to establish an audience. Many of TV's best-loved classics would never have made it to a second series in today's environment.

Yet *Dark Shadows* looks set to rise from the grave once more, courtesy of two of its most influential fans – with cult director Tim Burton at the helm and Johnny Depp starring in a big-screen version, pencilled for release in 2011. 'Dark Shadows is happening,' confirmed Depp in a recent interview. 'It's exciting, very exciting. It's like a lifelong dream for me. I loved the show when I was a kid. I was obsessed with Barnabas Collins. I have photographs of me holding Barnabas Collins posters when I was five or six. I'm very excited to do it.' 'There was something very weird about [*Dark Shadows*], it had the weirdest vibe to it,' says fellow fan Burton. 'I'm sort of intrigued about that vibe. It's early days on it, but I'm excited about it.' 'For me, all other vampires paled when compared to Barnabas,' said Thane Burnett, a journalist who adored the show as a kid and was inspired to track down its original star after news of the Depp/Burton remake. 'Critics dismissed *Dark Shadows* as campy. But fans – who gather still for *Dark Shadows* conventions – recognised Barnabas as a figure with heart. However unbeating...'

Dracula Prince of Darkness

Barbara Shelley as Helen Kent in *Dracula Prince of Darkness*

'The greatest all new fright show in town!'

A beautiful woman glides through the dappled shadows of Castle Dracula's great hall, a spectral vision in white. Her long auburn hair cascades down to her shoulders, drawing attention to her porcelain-pale cleavage – laid tantalisingly bare by the plunging neckline of her flimsy Victorian nightdress. Her sister-in-law Diana cannot quite believe her eyes as the white lady approaches. This can't be Helen, the dowdy prude she knows so well, this voluptuous creature beckoning her with velvet words and a suggestive smirk. As she draws closer the air crackles with the promise of a taboo embrace. Helen's lips part to reveal delicate fangs and her eyes sparkle with unholy hunger. To the audience's mixed disappointment and relief, the spell is broken as Dracula appears at the head of the stairs, hissing with rage, to claim Diana for himself. 'Helen is the epitome of evil, a frightened lady who becomes the victim of vicious sexuality,' says Barbara Shelley, the actress who plays the part in 1966's *Dracula: Prince of Darkness*.

The prim and proper Victorian matron – all buttoned-up blouses and starched frocks – who, after experiencing the kiss of evil, becomes a lethal and lascivious, spitting sex kitten. It's the essence of vampirism as immortalised by Hammer – a frightening contagion that unleashes the libido, wreaking havoc with repressed matrimonial harmony; the vampire's curse as an ambivalent blessing, acting on its victims in the manner of a Satanic aphrodisiac. Few actresses embody this sexual transformation better than Barbara Shelley, as the priggish Helen Kent, who becomes a sensual demon after experiencing the unholy embrace of Christopher Lee's Count in *Dracula: Prince of Darkness*. The transformation has much in common with the clichéd scene of the bespectacled librarian, who literally lets her hair down, taking off her glasses to reveal a secret sexy side in countless cheesy romantic comedies and tacky soft porn flicks.

Barbara Shelley takes this familiar formula up a step in *Dracula: Prince of Darkness*, in which her character not only lets her hair down, but grows a set of wicked incisors to match, discarding her inhibitions under the unholy influence of the Count. The film

The beautiful British character actress Barbara Shelley as the ill-fated tourist Helen Kent in Dracula: Prince of Darkness was directed by Terence Fisher, who helmed both *The Horror of Dracula* and *The Curse of Frankenstein*. Launching Hammer's impressive string of Gothic films in the '50s, he's responsible for many of the most memorable horror pictures produced by the studio in the wake of these two movies. Fisher has subsequently downplayed his contribution, expressing little interest in the horror genre. But the popularity of his films has led critics to re-evaluate the director's influence and style, some of whom have detected elements of Victorian values in the director's period chillers.

Most identify Fisher's horror flicks as adult fairytales with strong moralistic undertones. Good and evil are clearly defined, with virtue invariably overcoming villainy. The picture is muddied however, since in Hammer's Technicolor universe, good tends to be staid and dull, while evil is dangerous and sexy. Barbara Shelley recalls asking Terence Fisher for guidance as to exactly how she should play Helen Kent once she's fallen under Dracula's curse. 'He said, "Just remember, a vampire will have anything that's not nailed down." That's how I tried to play it.' It's also how countless (pun intended) other female vampires have played it since, and while the self-deprecating Miss Shelley may give credit for her performance to her director, it is her interpretation of the role that set the standard for future wilting Gothic heroines, destined to fall from grace after a brush with supernatural evil.

'I only played one vampire, but nobody believes that!' says the actress of the enduring cult status of her most influential performance. 'It's so real to you when you're playing it. In *Dracula: Prince of Darkness*, when I played the vampire, I had in my mind the feeling of a Greek fury. I talked to darling Terry Fisher, who reckoned that the vampire was basically evil. I thought, "Okay, something that's ranting and raving, and carrying on within itself," and I thought of a fury from reading the old Greek tragedies and dramas. I always like to have what I call a peg to hang my hat on. Once I've found it, it's mine – but I've got to find that peg, first of all.'

Picking just one definitive vampire vixen from Hammer's distinguished roll call of fanged femmes is no easy task. As the studio's hugely successful recipe of Gothic chills and titillating thrills developed, Hammer recruited some of the sexiest women to adorn the silver screen in the '60s in order to deliver the glamour their audiences came to expect. Barbara Shelley's predecessors in Hammer's 1958 *Dracula* – Valerie Gaunt as the Count's Bride and Melissa Stribling as his willing victim Mina – give sterling performances, but the film belongs to Christopher Lee's portrayal of the Count. By way of comparison, Barbara's Helen steals the show, in part because Lee refused to utter a line of the script of *Dracula: Prince of Darkness*, but mostly thanks to Shelley's sudden shift from nervous English wallflower to undead man-eater. Switching effortlessly between the two, she makes the change compelling, sexy and utterly convincing.

'Nothing's wrong. Come sister ... You don't need Charles.'

It's also a daring part. There's no mistaking the lesbian overtones of Helen's attempt to sink her teeth into her sister-in-law Diana, which was shocking stuff then, even

Associated British-Pathé Ltd present A Hammer Film Production
"DRACULA—PRINCE OF DARKNESS"
STARRING (X)
CHRISTOPHER LEE
BARBARA SHELLEY   ANDREW KEIR
TECHNISCOPE (R)   TECHNICOLOR (R)
RELEASED THROUGH WARNER-PATHE DISTRIBUTORS LTD

Helen is menaced by her mysterious host – none other than Count Dracula.

for the swinging '60s. Discussing the role at the time, Shelley observed that it might not do her profile any good, though it was at least testament to the fact that, 'I'm not particularly obsessed with preserving a public image, or being a starry girl.' By the '70s, soft-core lesbianism had become a regular standby in Hammer's vampire flicks, while studio executives began to spend as much time leafing through *Playboy* as consulting theatrical agents when looking for talent to lend glamour to their next Gothic chiller. Loosening censorship meant audiences were demanding more than mere suggestiveness from Hammer, who in turn required their actresses to bare increasing amounts of skin in order to qualify for their roles.

Nastassja Kinski, female star of *To the Devil a Daughter*, bared all for the camera in 1976, yet this film turned out to be Hammer's last – an indication that it was sensual titillation, rather than blatant sex scenes, that lent Hammer's Gothic pictures their unique, erotic charm. Barbara Shelley herself was always careful to draw the line when called upon to disrobe for her art. In her first horror film, *Cat Girl*, Barbara took special precautions to avoid the camera taking advantage of her. 'There was a scene where I was sitting up in bed,' she recalled in *Hammer Glamour*. 'I got the hairdresser to write "stop" across the top of my chest, so when I sat up and dropped the sheet I knew it couldn't be seen to go too far.' When the producers of *Blood of the Vampire* – a film designed to cash in on the success of Hammer's *Horror of Dracula* – tried to pressurise her into a nude scene not in her contract, Barbara refused, saying that they could sue her, but that if they

The bite of the Count (played here by Christopher Lee) unleashes unholy sexual urges in his victims in Hammer's Dracula *films.*

later cut in scenes with a body double to give the impression she'd gone through with it, she'd be the one suing them.

'Hammer knew that it wasn't what you saw that was important, it was what you *didn't* see,' she said of her role in *Dracula: Prince of Darkness*. In this instance, the actress was referring to the gore in the film. In one of the most infamous scenes, her unconscious husband is hoisted up over Dracula's coffin and his throat slit, so that the resultant cascade of blood will revive the Count. The sequence repelled many critics, some of whom even insisted that the victim was gutted while hanging helpless over the stone sarcophagus – a triumph of suggestive direction lent extra power by Shelley's horrified response upon discovering her exsanguinated husband. The same principle applies to the sexual aspects of the film, the faintest suggestion of sexual hunger in Helen's eyes lending the film an erotic charge more powerful than any throwaway topless shot.

'There'll be no morning for us.'

That is not, of course, to suggest that the actresses who followed in Barbara's footsteps, willing to expose more than a flash of cleavage at Hammer's request, were not sexy. We've already paid tribute to the inimitable Ingrid Pitt, whose unabashed nudity made her the definitive Hammer sex kitten in many eyes, and the other nubile actresses and models who set the screen alight for the studio by baring their charms on camera. But Barbara Shelley wasn't alone among Hammer starlets in maintaining her modesty without compromising her screen-siren credentials. Actresses Yvonne Romain (*Curse of the Werewolf*) and Valerie Leon (*Blood from the Mummy's Tomb*) are still revered as scream queens among Hammer fans despite refusing to reveal all in their sexy starring roles. 'Somebody did a little book about me once called *Everything but the Nipple*,' said Leon, 'and the title came from the fact that I always showed a lot of cleavage but nothing else. I believe that suggestion is far more titillating.'

Barbara Shelley also enjoys cult status as one of Hammer's most prolific female stars. Despite languishing under leading lights like Christopher Lee and Peter Cushing on the billboards, her performances remain integral to many of the studio's finest films. In other productions besides *Dracula: Prince of Darkness*, she takes the role of the repressed prude, given a new lust for life by an erotic exposure to evil. In *Rasputin: The Mad Monk* – filmed back-to-back with *Dracula: Prince of Darkness* on many of the same sets – she appears as a respectable lady who becomes obsessed with the maverick Russian mystic (played by Christopher Lee). In *The Gorgon*, she's a glamorous assistant to Dr Namaroff (Peter Cushing), unaware that the full moon turns her into the hideous snake-haired demon of Greek mythology. In Hammer's acclaimed science-fiction shocker *Quatermass and the Pit*, she plays the scientist Miss Judd, who offers a telepathic window into the distant past, when demonic Martians ruled the earth. The variety of roles taken on by Barbara Shelley in these Hammer movies – just a few in her distinguished screen career – is indicative of her range as an actress, and key to her enduring allure as the silver screen's greatest victim turned vamp.

Playing a truly immortal daughter of darkness takes more than just curves and a pretty face. Talent and charm are essential, and Barbara's many performances have earned her a special place in the affections of discerning film aficionados – particularly those with a taste for horror. On the subject of the dark fascination of the vampire, the actress is typically self-effacing. 'As to the eroticism of the legend, so much has already been said and written on that subject by people far more capable than I that I can add very little,' she says. 'Perhaps the eroticism is heightened by the night symbols, and by the unbridled greed and determination of the vampire to achieve its ends. There is always something fascinating and repellent about a completely uncontrolled and rabid emotion.' Something that becomes even more fascinating – and exciting – when the disintegration of control and liberation of sensuality is depicted with the old-school charm and subtle eroticism Barbara Shelley brings to her portrayal of Helen Kent, surely Dracula's classiest conquest yet.

Black Sunday

Barbara Steele as Princess Asa Vajda in *Black Sunday*

'Stare into these eyes. You will be dead to man ... but alive in death!'

It must be one of the most memorable and exciting opening sequences in the history of horror cinema. It is the seventeenth century in Moldavia, the ancient Eastern European principality bordering Transylvania. Princess Asa Vajda is being tried for sorcery, alongside her brother and lover Javuto. Making it a family affair, the inquisitor who pronounces death upon the duo is also her brother. Filial sentiment clearly plays no part in the Grand Inquisitor's sentence. The princess's back is branded with an 'S', marking her out as a servant of Satan, and the mask of Satan is placed over face. A grotesque, bronze device, lined with wicked spikes, horror-stricken viewers can only imagine the princess's excruciating agony as a brawny, hooded executioner literally hammers it onto her terrified features with the aid of a huge wooden mallet. Before the mask could be put in place, however, Asa had vowed revenge from beyond the grave in the name of her master the Devil. To the terror of the assembled court, after she dies, a mighty storm whips up, putting out the fire before it can reduce her body to ashes.

The sequence's impact is amplified by Barbara Steele's performance as Asa. Her strange beauty makes the horrific sight of the hideous bronze mask being nailed to the witch's face even more disturbing. The unearthly spite ominously lurking beneath that beauty renders her curse just as chilling. The powerful prologue proves a hard act to follow, but it's a tribute to the film's director, Mario Bava, that the atmosphere and chills seldom let up, even after the action moves 200 hundred years later. *Black Sunday*, made in 1960 and also known as *The Mask of Satan*, is now widely recognised as a masterpiece, not just of Italian Gothic filmmaking, but a milestone in horror, and indeed cinema history. Much of the credit must go to Bava as a brilliant visual stylist, capable of weaving a powerful and eerie spell with his peerless cinematography, despite some less than special effects and hackneyed dialogue. But the film's focus rests very much upon the haunting presence of its female star, particularly her eyes – with posters for *Black Sunday* focusing on Barbara Steele's most striking feature, entreating potential patrons to 'stare into these eyes'.

In the film, she takes on two roles – both the evil Asa, who rises from the grave

The delicate features of Barbara Steele, about to disappear beneath the mask of Satan.

thirsting for vengeance; and her descendent, the virtuous Katia, who Asa plans to possess as part of her evil scheme. This dual role emphasises Barbara's unique quality, the weird ambivalence of her appearance. Almost doll-like in her smouldering beauty, she manages to combine a look of angelic innocence with a suggestion of devilish malevolence. 'A strange type was needed, and we chose Steele from pictures,' said Bava of casting *Black Sunday*, later explaining that Steele 'had the perfect face for my films'. 'In later years she would sigh that though *Black Sunday* was undoubtedly a masterpiece of poetic horror, it was a cinematographer's vision through and through; the girl on screen could have been anyone,' writes the celebrated film journalist Maitland McDonagh in her essay 'The Face that Launched a Thousand Screams: Barbara Steele'. 'In this Steele is thoroughly mistaken. The girl onscreen could have been no one else.'

There is something elusive about Barbara Steele's spectral charm, something even her many fans find difficult to pin down. 'By all rights, Barbara Steele's face should be kittenish: the high, wide forehead; the huge, round eyes; the tiny tapered chin. But it's nothing of the kind,' observes McDonagh. 'It's a pale, angular mask as hard and polished as her name. Steele's face is simultaneously alluring and alarming, never cute. Critic Raymond Durgnat once declared that Steele's very eyelids snarl, and the late Italian director Riccardo Freda, who worked with her twice, rhapsodised that "in certain conditions of light and colour, her face assumes a cast that doesn't appear to be quite human".' In the years following the success of *Black Sunday*, Barbara Steele would work with some of the greatest cult horror directors of the era – not just Italians like Bava and Freda, but also celebrated English directors like Michael Reeve and Americans like Roger Corman.

Barbara was born in England, and began her acting career appearing in a few long-forgotten British films, before pursuing her fortune in Hollywood. She was offered a part playing opposite Elvis Presley in the film *Blazing Star*. In preparation, studio image-makers dyed her hair and instructed her to get a tan, which was going markedly against the grain for the spirited English actress. Before the cameras started rolling, she was off the project. 'I felt like a total lie as a blonde, because it didn't suit my nature, which is pretty dark,' Steele later reflected. 'And I said to myself, "I'm out of here."'

Next stop was Rome, where the Italian film industry was enjoying a renaissance, producing films that were often more stylish and daring than their Hollywood equivalents. 'I find it very interesting that, in this great period of phenomenal optimism in Italy, these horror movies came out, because the dark side is always going to express itself somewhere,' she says. 'And the kick-off was *Black Sunday*!'

'You, too, can feel the joy and happiness of Hades.'

Producers gave Bava an unusually generous budget for *Black Sunday* by the low-budget standards of the Italian cinema of the day. Nonetheless, the shoot was not without its problems. 'We had hardly any idea what was going down on that film,' recalls Barbara of the film's ad hoc script. 'We had no idea of the end, or the beginning either, not at all.' Steele herself could be tricky, with Bava recalling that the actress was 'superstitious,

afraid of Italians. She refused to come to the set because someone had told her I was using a special film stock that, when developed, made the actors look naked! Maybe she misunderstood someone who told her I did camera tricks, or something like that. I reassured the poor woman by saying that if I'd had such an invention, I'd have made millions long ago.'

'Lord alone knows, I was difficult enough,' Barbara later confessed. 'I didn't like my fangs – I had them changed three times. I loathed my wig – I changed that four times. I couldn't understand Italian... I certainly didn't want to allow them to tear open my dress and expose my breasts, so they got a double that I didn't like at all, so I ended up doing it myself – drunk, barely over eighteen, embarrassed, and not very easy to be around.' Some of that maverick spirit no doubt contributed to her memorable performance (while the director later decided to dispense with the fangs entirely, as they looked hokey on film). The actress recalls that filming *Black Sunday* also had a weird ambience. 'Film is so porous, and to my mind so occult, that I think film itself absorbs odd energies like a living skin,' ponders Barbara. In particular, the black and white of the film seemed to echo eerily on the set, which she remembers being 'so monochromatic that nobody, not even a crew member, wore a single colour on the set – hypnotically beautiful, shrouded in fog, luminous and incandescent, with all the elements of a religious manifestation'.

Black Sunday was a minor hit in Italy and a major hit abroad, particularly in America, where it was distributed by AIP. The film was strong stuff by the standards of the day and was banned until 1968 by censors in the UK. AIP toned down several aspects of the film, cutting back some of the grislier scenes and altering dialogue to remove the suggestion of an incestuous relationship between Asa and Javuto, who they changed into the Princess's servant in a newly-dubbed soundtrack. Asa's boast that 'you, too, can feel the joy and happiness of Hades' was changed to 'the happiness of hating' for the US cut. The critics, overall, were impressed, one describing *Black Sunday* as 'the most original vampire tale since Bela Lugosi's *Dracula*'. The *New York Times*' Eugene Archer hated the film, noting ambivalently that, 'Barbara Steele, a blank-eyed manikin with an earthbound figure and a voice from outer space, is appropriately cast as a vampire.'

Most importantly, however, audiences loved it, making it AIP's most successful film at that point. They'd also recently had a big hit with an adaptation of Edgar Allan Poe's wonderfully Gothic short story, 'The Fall of the House of Usher', stylishly directed by Roger Corman and starring the peerless horror icon Vincent Price. Sensing they might have a winning formula on their hands, the studio hired Steele to star opposite Price in Corman's next Poe adaptation, *The Pit and the Pendulum*. Steele and Price did not get on particularly well by all accounts – her youthful high spirits grating on Price's conservative professionalism – but, in common with many directors, Roger Corman identified something unique in his leading lady. 'There was a depth to her,' he said. 'On the surface she was a beautiful brunette [...] beneath that – and you could almost get poetic here – looking into her eyes, you could see layer upon layer. I could probably best, inadequately, describe it as a kind of exotic mystery.'

The actress went on to carve herself a career as a cult actress, primarily in a number of further low-budget European horror flicks – not one of which matched the quality or impact of *Black Sunday*. 'I usually played these roles where I represented the dark side,' reflects Barbara. 'I was always a predatory bitch goddess in all of these movies, with all kinds of unspeakable elements of necrophilia and rising from the dead and perpetuating curses. The women that I played were usually very powerful women and they suffered for it. You saw these powerful women – usually adulteresses, full of lust and greed, playing out all this repressed stuff – and then in the end I always seemed to get it. And there was always this sort of morality play, this sort of final pay-off, and that was very consoling to everybody, because the dark goddess can't just go on wreaking havoc *ad infinitum*. She gets her comeuppance, too.'

'Look into my eyes! Come closer ... Just a few drops of your blood brought me to life again. All of your blood will give me the strength to accomplish my vengeance. Come, kiss me!'

By the '70s, Barbara's career had gone into decline. Since then, she's gone on record more than once regarding her early horror roles, revealing sentiments that are ambivalent to say the least. 'We had a marvellous time,' admits the actress. 'The only thing I resent – because it is a bloody difficult genre – is that these films can stop you from doing others because of the terrible image bag they get you into. They were all made very quickly, too. We'd work with three cameras for sixteen hours a day. It was a good job they were horror films – a girl can't do close-ups after sixteen hours! Seriously, any script – any circumstance – that is not believable, is much more difficult to do, to make something happen, than a more realistic drama. I got superstitious about the films, too. I may not believe in fate, but those pictures were a bit chancy, a little spooky. I swear I'm never going to climb out of another bloody coffin as long as I live!'

The English rose's attitude to her cult status in horror fandom has softened over the years. She even accepted the role of Dr Hoffman – who Barbara describes as 'sort of a deranged alchemist' – in the ill-fated 1991 attempt to revive Gothic soap opera *Dark*

In Black Sunday, *director Mario Bava created a dreamlike atmosphere of Gothic dread that has influenced numerous subsequent filmmakers.*

Shadows. *Black Sunday*'s reputation has built over the years and it has been cited as a formative influence on Francis Ford Coppola's 1992 movie *Bram Stoker's Dracula*. Tim Burton, arguably the most influential director to devote himself to the Gothic aesthetic, named *Black Sunday* as his own favourite film and the movie that made the greatest impact upon him as a child. 'Once you see Barbara Steele, you know you will never forget her,' says Burton. 'She is probably one of the only real horror goddesses. There is a timelessness that she has.' Perhaps the closest equivalent to Barbara Steele in contemporary Hollywood is Christina Ricci. The likeness seems particularly apparent in *Sleepy Hollow* (1999), Tim Burton's most overt tribute to old-school Gothic cinema yet.

Burton paid tribute to Bava's Gothic opus. 'The vibe and the feeling is what it's about,' he points out. 'A mixture of eroticism, of sex, of horror and starkness of image – and to me that is more real than what most people would consider realism in films.'

'There was always a high level of sexuality in every horror film,' adds Steele, 'because you are dealing with death and very primal things and you've always got to have this juxtaposition of a subtext, of a very powerful, sexual subtext, whatever is going on. I mean, you try and invest it with a kind of force.'

'We dream of her haunted gaze and her razor-sharp cheekbones floating eerily in the perpetual gothic darkness; we cherish her creamy, marble-white bosom and her lethal legs,' gushes Maitland McDonagh, waxing lyrical on Barbara's inimitably fatal charms. 'Who but Steele could have looked so hauntingly seductive with nail punctures dotting her face? And who but Steele could have brought such haughty grace to films with such kinky underpinnings?' A reluctant horror queen she may be, but Barbara Steele remains one of the most haunting presences in cult cinema – uncanny and eerie, yet strangely seductive, a French magazine has aptly dubbed her, 'Marilyn for the disciples of Count Dracula'.

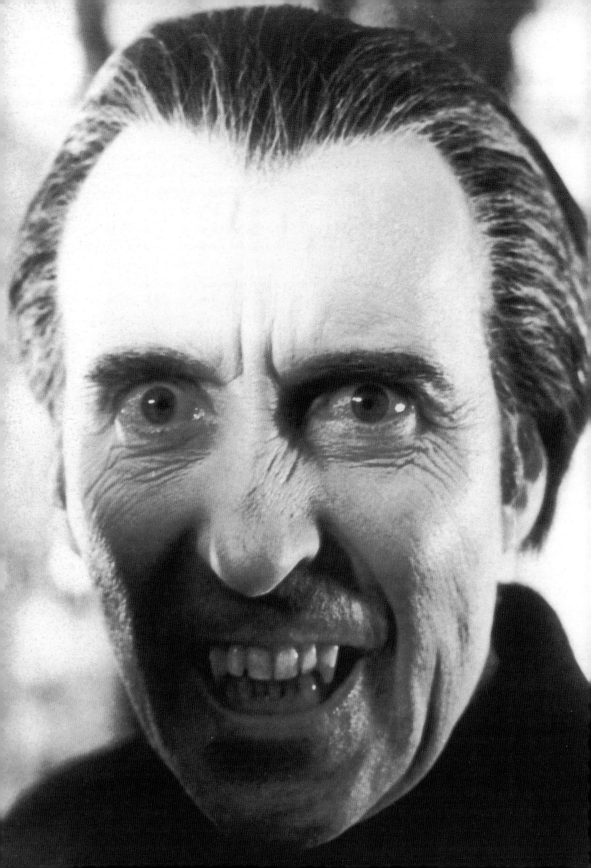

Christopher Lee as
Count Dracula in *The Horror of Dracula*

The terrifying lover, who died – yet lived!

At the top of Castle Dracula's stone staircase, a dark presence looms, and Jonathan Harker's sense of quietly building dread is shared by virtually every audience member. Indeed, nobody who attended the first screenings of *The Horror of Dracula* in 1958 knew quite what to expect as the imposing cloaked figure emerged from the shadows. That first glimpse of Christopher Lee as Dracula is a cinematic moment as immortal as the vampire Count himself. The very personification of saturnine power, of mannered menace, he catches Harker off guard. This is no monster – at least, not in the conventional sense – but something far more threatening. Dracula greets his guest with casual charm, his richly sonorous voice complimenting the tall, dignified poise of this black-clad host perfectly. His appearance sends a shudder down Harker's spine that reverberated among audiences across the world. A shudder not just of fear, but of something altogether more ambivalent – something approaching curious anticipation – particularly among the female cinemagoers of the 1950s...

This memorable slice of cinematic magic saw Christopher Lee's Count throw a shadow not just over Jonathan Harker (played here by John Van Eyssen), and *The Horror of Dracula*'s eager early audiences, but the whole of Gothic cinema thereafter. The popular image of Dracula was changed forever. For over 25 years, when people thought of Dracula, they'd conjured Bela Lugosi's classic portrayal of the Count as a reptilian Eastern European with slicked-back hair and a sinister leer. Christopher Lee stole the Hungarian actor's crown, becoming the definitive Dracula for a new generation – a virile, lupine aristocrat, able to cow mere mortals with a single withering stare. It's a tribute to the lasting power of Lee's performance, that even though the Count may not seem as spine-chilling as he first did during that career-defining debut, his Dracula still endures as the classic interpretation over 50 years later.

In 2009 *Entertainment Weekly* made him their second greatest vampire ever ('Lee will always be remembered – especially by cowering beauties in their gauzy negligées – for his suave, silent, and really, really thirsty Count Dracula'), a position he also occupies

Christopher Lee – still the definitive Dracula in the eyes of many fans.

in the *SFX* poll. ('Put that down to being the quintessential English gentleman – but with something of the night about him,' notes the magazine. 'And pure, unadulterated quality.') But just what – aside from his imposing height – makes Christopher Lee such a towering presence in the vampire stakes? At the time, the actor insisted he was bemused at the flood of admiring female fan mail that followed his debut as the world's most distinguished vampire. 'I'm frankly puzzled,' Christopher told one reporter in 1958, dismissing it as 'an odd sex manifestation. Maybe it's because I tried to make Dracula a romantic and tragic figure. Someone you could feel sorry for.'

'I am Dracula and I welcome you to my house.'

'Neither [director] Terence Fisher nor anyone else really knew how to present the character,' revealed Lee. 'I had read the book and I thought, "Here's a man who is romantic, erotic and heroic: that's the way I should play him."' Even if Fisher had his doubts as to how the Count should be portrayed on screen, the director seems to have been pretty clear on other matters – not least, the vamp's effect upon his victims. 'When she arrived back after having been away all night, she said it all in one close-up by the door,' said Fisher of Melissa Stribling's performance as one of Dracula's less-than-reluctant conquests. 'She'd been gone the whole night through! I remember Melissa Stribling saying, "Terry, how should I play this scene?" So I told her, "Listen, you should imagine you've just had one whale of a sexual night – the best one of your whole sexual experience. Give me that in your face!"'

The *Horror of Dracula* was the second Gothic chiller directed by Terence Fisher with Hammer's backing. It was known simply as *Dracula* in its British homeland, the longer title adopted for fear of legal action from the US studio Universal, who produced the Lugosi *Dracula* in 1931. Hammer had already enjoyed a surprise success with *The Curse of Frankenstein* in 1957, and so a film devoted to the vampire Count was the obvious follow-up. Hammer's fresh interpretations of these classic Gothic sagas truly rang the changes. Not only were they filmed in colour, they also introduced lashings of Kensington Gore – the theatrical blood favoured in productions of the day – which shocked contemporary critics, even if it looks terribly tame by modern standards. The studio's evolving house style involved creating its own distinctive atmosphere – a Victorian Central European fantasyland of cobwebbed crypts and bucolic graveyards, of quaint village inns and sinister Gothic castles, surrounded by endless forests. It's a world that has as much in common with Grimm's fairytales as the more visceral horror that followed in Hammer's wake.

Into this self-contained world of Gothic fantasy, reality seldom intrudes, and so within this space the taboo mysteries of sex and violence could be explored in safety. The films were made on tight budgets, and the perils depicted are normally to the sanctity of the family or the innocence of individuals rather than the world-shaking threats found in

This promotional shot from The Horror of Dracula *has become one of the most iconic images in horror cinema.*

Above: The Count greets his victim. Below: Making off into the night with his eager conquest.

grander productions. In *The Horror of Dracula*, large parts of the original novel are cut, as was the Count's ability to change shape. The latter had the effect not only of reducing production costs, but making the character of Dracula seem somewhat more plausible. Indeed, in Hammer's first Dracula film, the Count possesses few of the paranormal powers attributed to vampires in other pictures. He is strong, but not supernaturally so. It is the steely strength of his will, rather than any physical power that gives Lee's Dracula his fearsome presence on screen, making the Count so compelling and magnetic a monster.

The Horror of Dracula is a lean, taut film that highlights the clash between good and evil as a personal conflict – a contest of wills – between and Christopher Lee's feral Count Dracula and Dr Van Helsing, played by Peter Cushing as a hawkish crusader. The film's intimate scale meant that its impact rests squarely on the shoulders of the two lead actors, and both deliver in spades. Certain classic characters are continually reinvented, with the creation of new versions to suit the tastes and values of different generations. Some are taken to our collective hearts; others fade from memory. (There are, of course, more than a few cult Draculas in this book – worthy of note, but who failed to make a lasting impact on pop culture.) We have had numerous versions of Sherlock Holmes, for example, though few can rival the popularity of Basil Rathbone's interpretation of the master detective from the 1940s. Each of the ten-plus actors to depict the BBC's well-loved time-traveller Doctor Who have their own ardent following, though fans' favoured Doctor is often the one they grew up with.

To return to our subject, however, perhaps cinematic Dracula is best compared with big-screen super-spy James Bond. While other versions of 007 have always had their fans, Sean Connery's interpretation of the character remains far and away the most popular. The Scottish actor played the character six times, between 1962 and '71. But of the five other Bonds, only Daniel Craig, the most recent incumbent, has come close to rivalling Connery as the definitive face of 007. The same might be said of Christopher Lee's Dracula. Only Gary Oldman has come even close to eclipsing Christopher as the quintessential Count, but polls confirm that Oldman's 1992 Dracula still lacks the intimidating, iconic status of Lee's performance.

There are other revealing parallels between Connery's Bond and Lee's Count. Christopher Lee's tenure as Dracula for Hammer studios closely matches Sean Connery's time as 007 for Eon Productions (Christopher donned the fangs seven times for Hammer between 1958 and '72). Connery's Bond and Lee's Count are both products of the same era of British filmmaking and, by extension, British society. There are striking resemblances between them. (Christopher Lee would play Bond's nemesis Scaramanga in *The Man with the Golden Gun* – though by this time 007 was played by Roger Moore – a villain who was the evil mirror image of Bond. Ian Fleming, who penned the original Bond novels, was Lee's cousin.) They are both unflappably suave and impeccably dressed in formal eveningwear. Both exude a dark, faintly animalistic magnetism. Both are envied by men and desired by women. This last factor lends both characters their worrying ambivalence, because at core, this appeal relates to the murderous brutality inherent in the nature of both 007 and Dracula.

Though seldom commented upon, it's difficult to imagine Sean Connery's interpretation passing muster in a modern movie, given this celebrated Bond's undeniably aggressive attitude towards women. Many of 007's seductions in the early Bond films appear worryingly close to sexual assault by today's standards. In *The Horror of Dracula*, the Count disciplines his Bride in a fashion that looks uncomfortably close to domestic violence. When Dracula is shown feeding upon his female prey in Hammer films, it is an act that hangs ominously between sensuality and savagery. His sighing victims might surrender to the Count's mesmeric power, but this sexual predator knows only hunger and has no interest in consent.

Of course, to equate the appeal of Christopher Lee's vampire with some kind of Gothic rape fantasy is both piously over-simplistic and an unwarranted insult to his many fans. But to ignore the aspects of the character that link dark sexuality with games of dominance and submission is to lose sight of the very essence of Christopher Lee's immortal Prince of Darkness.

Lee complained that the thick contact lenses Hammer's special-effects department designed for his character became increasingly painful to wear.

At core, the character is about power in all its forms – sexual, physical, supernatural… even social. While few interpretations of the Count wholly ignore the aristocratic heritage implicit in his title, none have captured his essential nobility quite like Christopher Lee. Lee himself claims a noble lineage, stretching back through his mother's side to the legendary Dark Age Emperor Charlemagne, and he invariably brings an air of stately gravitas to every scene he plays. 'Above all, I have never forgotten that Count Dracula was a gentleman, a member of the upper aristocracy, and in his early life a great soldier and leader of men,' says Lee of his portrayal of the Prince of Darkness. True nobility is all about blood. Not just the intermarriage that takes place among the lofty heights of every ancient family tree, but also the violence that lies buried at its roots.

Trace any noble family back far enough and you'll discover that they almost unfailingly seized their birthright by force, imposing their right to rule with a mailed fist. Nobility can imply not just etiquette and breeding, but oppression and power. Christopher Lee's Count captures that contrast, of a man – or at least something that was once a man –

who conceals the cruel instincts of a warrior, or even a beast, beneath a smooth, cultured façade. 'I saw him as aloof, dignified and austere, exploding into tigerish activity when necessary,' said the actor – a commanding contradiction his growing legion of female fans found fascinating. It also gave Lee's Dracula an element of depth lacking from so many other interpretations.

You would play your brains against mine... against me who has commanded nations!

It is nothing short of remarkable that he does this with such economy, dominating not just the film, but the future of Gothic cinema with a little over five minutes total screen time and less than twenty lines of dialogue. (Indeed, he has so little dialogue that the second quote in this profile is actually drawn from his performance in *Dracula A.D. 1972*.) The actor was well aware of the power of the role of Dracula – it had fatally typecast his predecessor Bela Lugosi – and was reluctant to revisit the performance for fear of suffering a similar fate. But *The Horror of Dracula* proved such a huge commercial hit that Hammer badgered him to appear in a sequel, Lee finally relenting six years later for *Dracula: Prince of Darkness*. He was deeply unhappy with the script, however, and refused to speak any of the lines, replacing them with glares and hisses. It's a tribute to Christopher's physical charisma that the Count remains such a mesmeric presence regardless.

Christopher Lee was perhaps right to be wary of his fanged alter-ego. With well over 250 films and TV shows under his belt, he has entered *The Guinness Book of Movie Facts & Feats* as being the international star with the most screen credits. Yet, despite this, he has only recently emerged from beneath the shadow of his most famous performance – something of a sore point for the actor, who openly dislikes discussing Dracula. Just as his Count dominates *The Horror of Dracula* despite minimal screen time, Dracula defines Lee's public persona, even though he only played the part a handful of times during a formidably long and prolific career. Now he has established himself in the consciousness of a new generation of fans courtesy of parts in two of Hollywood's most successful franchises – *Star Wars* and *The Lord of the Rings* – perhaps Lee can finally look a little more kindly on his most immortal creation. Certainly, as far as many vampire fans are concerned, Christopher Lee's imperious Count – an inimitable creature of darkly dignified sexual savagery – remains cinema's definitive Dracula.

Dracula's Daughter

Gloria Holden as Countess Marya Zaleska in *Dracula's Daughter*

'She gives you that weird feeling!'

An elegantly austere figure, swathed in black, presides over a pyre on the mist-wreathed Yorkshire moors. There is no mistaking her nobility from her stately bearing; any more than one could mistake this sombre gathering for anything other than a funeral, though there are but two mourners in attendance. 'Unto Adonai and Azrael, into the keeping of the lords of the flaming lower pits, I consign this body to be forevermore consumed in this purging fire,' she intones in a crisp, evocative voice. 'Let all baleful spirits that threaten the souls of men be banished by the sprinkling of this salt. Be thou exorcised, O Dracula, and thy body long undead find destruction throughout eternity in the name of thy dark, unholy master.' At this she brandishes a crude wooden crucifix, though it causes both her and her companion to flinch. 'In the name of the all holies and through this cross, be the evil spirit cast out until the end of time.'

'Free, free forever,' she exults at the conclusion of the ceremony. 'Do you understand what that means, Sandor? Free to live as a woman, free to take my place in the bright world of the living instead of among the shadows of the dead.' 'Perhaps,' her strange servant Sandor responds grimly.

The lady is Countess Marya Zaleska; the corpse she has just cremated that of her father, the legendary Count Dracula. The plot of *Dracula's Daughter* follows immediately on from Universal's classic *Dracula*, though it took five years before the studio filmed this sequel to their 1931 blockbuster. Bela Lugosi, the original Count, appears only briefly in effigy in the film, as a corpse in the above scene (though he was apparently paid more for not appearing in this film than he was for his performance in *Dracula*).

Certainly the Countess is something of a chip off the old tombstone. Marya, as played by the London-born actress Gloria Holden, is pale and sepulchral in appearance, oozing aloof, aristocratic menace with carefully-plucked bat-wing eyebrows over an inscrutable, imperious gaze. She wears a cape, but unlike Bela's old-fashioned opera cloak, Countess Zaleska's is a hooded modish affair that wouldn't look out of place hanging in the cloakroom at one of the trendy cocktail parties she attends. The rest of the Countess's wardrobe is

Gloria Holden takes on the role of the last of the line in Dracula's Daughter.

similarly sombrely stylish and subtly weird – particularly a bizarre grey gown, emphasising her bust, which some critics have compared to the post-mortem wrapping of a mummy.

She echoes the immortal line spoken by her fictional father when refusing red wine in *Dracula* – 'thank you, I never drink... wine' – though this time it is after being offered a glass of sherry at a fashionable soirée (and she is later seen demurely sipping a nice cup of tea). Countess Zaleska is the missing link between Dracula's Brides – his harem of shroud-clad 'sisters' who drift across the screen in *Dracula*'s early scenes – and the spirited undead hellcats who hiss and pout hungrily throughout the vampire flicks of the colour era. Gloria Holden's Marya would never lower herself to physically attacking her victims – she has a servant, Sandor, for that. Rather, the Countess procures the warm human blood she craves through hypnosis, or the deference due to her own blue blood. She exudes all of the authority of her status – a commanding, distant figure, with strange tastes that extend beyond her passion for playing haunting music and painting unsettling canvases. In a nod to the building fashion for Freudian psychology in the era, it is hinted that Marya's vampirism may be as much a psychiatric condition as a supernatural one, her principal foil being the psychiatrist Dr Jeffrey Garth (somewhat oafishly played as the hero by Otto Kruger).

> 'There are more things in heaven and earth than are
> dreamed of in your psychiatry, Mr Garth.'

The plot of *Dracula's Daughter* is primarily concerned with the Countess's attempt to escape the family curse. As such it represents a cinematic milestone in vampire lore: the first instance of the reluctant vampire, as much a victim of their unholy condition as those they kill. In contrast with Bela Lugosi's Count, who revels in his undead power, Countess Zaleska apparently just wants to be normal. At this point, the horror genre still enjoyed very little prestige in critical circles – most either dismissed horror movies as ludicrous or condemned them as disgusting. Some have suggested this helped lend power to Gloria Holden's portrayal of the Countess. She was reluctant to take the role of Marya, and that reluctance and disdain for the part translates well into the Countess's disgust at her own tainted heritage on the screen.

Even if she did make for a reluctant vampire, Gloria Holden's performance as Countess Zaleska – her first starring role – would be the one she was remembered for. It also earned her some plaudits in the press of the day. 'Gloria Holden is a remarkably convincing bat-woman,' conceded the *New York Times*, 'but we found ourselves wondering all the way through the picture how she managed to preserve so attractive an appearance – after sleeping in coffins and all – without the aid of a mirror.' On a less jokey note, the *Hollywood Spectator* observed that 'the student of cinema will find a wealth of study material in the penetratingly intelligent synthesis of Ms Gloria Holden... Her work bears the stamp of unguessable abilities.' Her performance also has its admirers today, some rating the film as far superior to Bela Lugosi's better-known *Dracula*. 'Gloria Holden, as the reluctant vampire protagonist, absolutely drips patrician eroticism,'

averred *Entertainment Weekly* in 2008. *Dracula's Daughter*'s most influential modern fan, however, is the authoress Anne Rice.

'My favourite vampire film will always be *Dracula's Daughter* with Gloria Holden,' she told journalist Aaron W. Tellock, 'which I saw as a child at the neighbourhood theatre and which I loved, for its treatment of the vampire as a tragic aristocrat, a person of sensibility and suffering.' While this romantic mood of doomed nobility certainly inspired one aspect of Anne Rice's immensely popular series of vampire novels, another that would become key in the authoress's *Vampire Chronicles* was a powerful undercurrent of homoeroticism. 'Gloria Holden in the title role almost single-handedly redefined the '20s movie vamp as an impressive Euro-butch dyke bloodsucker,' writes Gary Morris of *Dracula's Daughter* in an essay on 'Queer Horror' for *Bright Lights Film Journal*. 'Scenes of her cruising the dark streets of London (cruising is the word) play with society's image of the lesbian as a soulless predator, but modern audiences will respond to Holden's striking, mask-like face and haunting, luminous eyes as the intoxicating essence of transgressive lesbian power.'

One modern audience member who certainly responded was *Entertainment Weekly*'s critic, who describes a scene where the Countess lures a desperate young girl named Lili back to her studio, ostensibly to model for her, as 'so hot it's impossible to imagine how it ever got past '30s censors'. In fact, it very nearly didn't. 'The present suggestion that [...] Lili poses in the nude will be changed,' insisted America's chief censor Joe Breen after seeing a draft of the script. 'She will be posing her neck and shoulders, and there will be no suggestion that she undresses, and there will be no exposure of her person. It was also stated that the present incomplete sequence will be followed by a scene in which Lili is taken to a hospital and there it will be definitely established that she has been attacked by a vampire. The whole sequence will be treated in such a way as to avoid any suggestion of perverse sexual desire on the part of Marya or of an attempted sexual attack by her upon Lili.'

'You won't object to removing your blouse, will you?'

This was just one element of *Dracula's Daughter* that attracted the unwelcome attentions of the American censors, who had instituted the PCA in 1934, requiring all movies to be awarded – or indeed, refused – a certificate based upon the suitability of their content. The film's struggles with increasingly stringent censors go a long way to explaining why it took Universal Studios so long to make a follow-up to their smash hit *Dracula* of 1931. In many respects, the turbulent pre-history of *Dracula's Daughter* is the fascinating story of the film that might have been, if prudes like Joe Breen hadn't been given final say on what moviegoers were allowed to see. John L. Balderston, the man Universal originally commissioned to write the film, appears to have had no idea of how puritanical the PCA would be, submitting scripts for their approval that clearly made Mr Breen's blood boil.

Above: This scene – in which the Countess mesmerises a model – was one of the most controversial in the film.
Below: Bela Lugosi earned more for appearing in effigy during the cremation scene than for starring in Dracula.

'The use of a female Vampire instead of a male gives us the chance to play up SEX and CRUELTY legitimately,' wrote Balderston of his initial idea for *Dracula's Daughter* in 1933. 'In *Dracula* these had to be almost eliminated… We profit by making Dracula's daughter amorous of her victims… The seduction of young men will be tolerated whereas we had to eliminate seduction of girls from the original as obviously censorable.' The scriptwriter proposed that the action take place in Castle Dracula while the Count was away in England. His daughter would be in charge in Dracula's absence, disciplining his Brides with whips and chains in true dominatrix style, taking an unholy delight in the acts of torture she inflicts upon her stepmothers and willing male victims. Unsurprisingly, the American censors rejected the entire story, with its heady cocktail of sado-masochism and supernatural eroticism, as unacceptable. British censors were equally unimpressed, fulminating that, '*Dracula's Daughter* would require half a dozen [...] languages to adequately express its beastliness.'

Another writer, R.C. Sherriff, was commissioned by Universal to pen a version of *Dracula's Daughter* that censors might consider. He wrote a script which depicted Dracula's origins in the Middle Ages, in which the cruel Count – played once again by Bela Lugosi – is cursed by a vengeful wizard. His decadent courtiers are transformed into pigs while Dracula is doomed to eternity as a member of the undead. Joe Breen gave Sherriff's version short shrift, huffing that 'there still remains in the script a flavour suggestive of a combination of sex and horror'. The censors' absurd demands included insisting that victims could not be bitten while reclining, only when sat upright on sturdy chairs, and that the girls rounded up by Dracula's men should be explicitly identified as being kidnapped to provide dancing partners for the Count's guests. The list went on, making it quite clear that Breen's objections were really to horror movies in general and vampire movies in particular. With time running out, Universal finally commissioned a third script from one Garrett Fort, whose version of *Dracula's Daughter*, which downplayed the supernatural, and made the Countess into a reluctant victim of her condition, finally managed to slip through the censors' net, and onto the screen in the form in which we can see it today.

Another film being shot simultaneously, which also endured significant problems from the censors, was *Mark of the Vampire*. In many respects, it might also make a claim for being an unofficial depiction of 'Dracula's daughter' – his illegitimate offspring perhaps. When Bela Lugosi learnt that Universal no longer required his presence on set for *Dracula's Daughter*, the actor accepted an offer from rival studio MGM to appear in their new horror picture. He plays Count Mora, though his costume and demeanour are clearly those of Dracula, only a frilly shirt really distinguishing Bela's character from his most famous role. The part of his undead daughter Luna was taken by the actress Carroll Borland, whose long dark hair, parted in the middle, full heavily made-up lips and striking eyebrows could represent the prototype for the classic Goth chick who began appearing in nightclubs some 50 years later. While neither Carroll nor Bela enjoy much screen time, she steals the show, particularly in a scene where Luna flies across the scene like a bat.

Evidence of the film's censorship problems can be found in *Mark of the Vampire*'s variable running times. The preview version is listed as lasting 80 minutes, while the film available today is only an hour long. Some of the cuts appear to have been weak efforts at comic relief, but others were made to placate the censors. 'I often spent evenings with [scriptwriter Guy Endore] and his wife, and we discussed books, demonology, vampirism – and the Dracula character in particular,' Carroll later recalled. 'In fact, Guy created both in his mind and in the first draft of the script a much more horrifying creature than that which finally appeared on the screen. He envisaged a completely new factor to the story. You may remember that, in the film, Lugosi's Count appears with a bullet hole in his forehead, which is never fully explained. Well, according to the original script the Count had committed a terrible sin which had lost him his chance of peace after death. He had committed incest with Luna, then strangled her and shot himself.

'This was to give the characters of the two vampires a value of horrid fascination,' added Carroll. 'It could hardly be mentioned, of course, and would have been difficult to even imply on the screen, but Guy was not at all happy when all his suggestions of a bad-child, worse-father relationship were dropped from the story.' If Joe Breen and the PCA were unwilling to entertain the sadomasochism implicit in *Dracula's Daughter*, then it's hardly a surprise that incest was unlikely to pass muster. To further dilute the impact of *Mark of the Vampire*, in the film's finale Count Mora and Luna are revealed as actors, posing as vampires. For this reason, perhaps, Carroll Borland's Luna must yield centre stage to Gloria Holden's Countess Marya as the silver screen's first undead pin-up, though both ladies offer iconic prototypes for the fanged sex kittens that would follow in their wake…

Dracula

Bela Lugosi as Count Dracula in *Dracula*

The story of the strangest passion
the world has ever known!'

I am Dracula,' intones Bela Lugosi's Count, his carefully enunciated accent thick as velvet, his malevolent moon of a face leering down at his nervous guest from the imposing stone staircase. These few moments, depicting the initial meeting between the vampire and Renfield (played by Dwight Frye) in the 1931 production of *Dracula*, introduced the world to one of the screen's most iconic figures. The slicked-back black hair, the pale face divided by a cruel slash of a mouth, the opera cloak, even the thick Hungarian accent – all of the characteristics that have dominated depictions of Dracula ever since were established by Bela in this fateful performance. It has, in effect, become the definitive vampiric uniform – as familiar to most of us as Santa's fur-trimmed crimson suit and other such iconic costumes – though it has little in common with author Bram Stoker's description of Dracula in the original novel. Bela Lugosi's Count, one of the most reptilian interpretations of the role to date, does at least retain much of the overripe menace of Stoker's creation.

Many subsequent versions have tended to soften the character, making the Count a romantic figure, even a tragic anti-hero. But Bela's Dracula is quite clearly a creature of pure evil, a smirking spider at the centre of some unseen supernatural web. More recent adaptations of the story have filled in the Count's background, inviting sympathy for the character, but diminishing his essentially inhuman nature. Everything about Lugosi's performance – from his overblown acting style to his curious manner of speech – lends an enigmatic, eerie quality to his career-defining Dracula… a figure who seems almost alien in his creepiness. Critics have since suggested that this was a happy accident, owing much to Lugosi's limitations as an actor (he overacts outrageously) and his feeble grasp of the English language. One enduring story is that his English was so bad that Lugosi was forced to learn his lines phonetically, with no real idea of what he was saying, which was what leant his vocal characterisation its notoriously weird, ponderously phrased quality.

*The spider spinning his web for the unwary fly…
The blood is the life, Mr Renfield.'*

Hungarian actor Bela Lugosi achieves immortality in the title role of Dracula.

Bela himself agreed that his Hungarian origins had helped transform him into a sinister figure, due to xenophobia in Hollywood. 'If my accent betrayed my foreign birth, it also stamped me as an enemy in the imagination of the producers,' he said. According to Bela, previous to arriving in the US as a political refugee, he had primarily played heartthrobs in theatrical productions in his native Hungary as well as a number of German films. 'The vampire was a complete change from the usual romantic characters I was playing,' he later insisted, 'but it was a success.' The Count's costume looks distinctively eccentric to modern eyes, the only obvious points of reference being a waiter, or perhaps more appropriately, an undertaker. But when *Dracula* debuted, it was easily identified as the dapper garb of a silent-era matinée idol, made menacing by Lugosi's unnerving presence. It's an image now so familiar as to have become a cliché – more often played for laughs than chills today. The film itself now warrants only a 'PG' rating on DVD. However, improbable as it might seem to modern horror fans – hardened by 'torture porn' and serial-killer sagas – to cinemagoers of the '30s, Bela's Count was a seriously scary proposition.

Like Frank Langella's 1979 *Dracula*, Lugosi's *Dracula* began as a successful stage play. 'When *Dracula* was first presented on Broadway there were members of all audiences who took it seriously,' the actor reminisced in 1951. 'People screamed and fainted. The first-aid staff were kept busy all the time. I did not dare to pretend to bite my victims' necks for fear of a hysterical reaction from the public. Nowadays the customers – even the children – know it all. They have seen plenty of horror films.'

The term 'horror film' was coined in the wake of the huge success of Bela's *Dracula* and a production of *Frankenstein*, both released in 1931. Previous to that, the general public were poorly acquainted with the Count – and indeed, the legend of the vampire itself. In addition to initiating audiences to the chills of an encounter with the undead, Lugosi was also responsible for introducing many twentieth-century cinemagoers to the delicious thrills of an encounter with the Prince of Darkness.

Just as modern audiences might have difficulty crediting the 1931 *Dracula* as scary, so many jaded contemporary vampire aficionados will find it even more difficult to see Bela Lugosi's Count as exotic and alluring. Yet in the actor's prime, *Dracula* also turned the Hungarian into something of a Gothic sex symbol. 'When I was playing Dracula on the stage, my audiences were women,' he later insisted in an interview. 'There were men, too. Escorts the women *had brought with them*. For reasons only their dark subconscious knew. In order to establish a subtle sex intimacy. 'Women wrote me letters,' added the actor. 'Ah, what letters women wrote me! Young girls. Women from seventeen to 30. Letters of a horrible hunger. *Asking me if I cared only for maiden's blood*. Asking me if I had done the play because I was in reality that sort of Thing. And through these letters, couched in terms of shuddering, transparent fear, there ran the hideous note of – *hope*. They hoped that I was *Dracula*. They hoped that my love was the love of *Dracula*. They gloated over the Thing they did not yet understand. It was the embrace of Death their subconscious was yearning for. Death, the final triumphant lover. It made me know that the women of America are unsatisfied, famished, craving sensation, even though it be the sensation of death draining the red blood of life.'

It's all magnificently overwrought stuff – a typical example of Bela's bombastic persona. Even his fans admit that the Hungarian could be a bit of ham, both on and off screen. He was a noted old-fashioned *bon viveur* with a weakness for fine cigars and pretty girls. The fact that there were no less than five Mrs Lugosis is proof that Bela's claims of his appeal to the fairer sex were more than idle boasts, though the most striking evidence of his unorthodox sex appeal came while he was touring with the stage version of *Dracula*. When the film star Clara Bow, Hollywood's leading sex symbol of the era, heard about the smash-hit play in 1928, she immediately secured tickets and dashed to see its enigmatic Hungarian lead in action. Not even troubling to dress, she just threw a mink coat on over her swimsuit. Clara was smitten, eagerly arranging to meet Bela backstage after the performance. The admiration was clearly mutual, and the unlikely couple embarked on a lengthy affair, Bela even commissioning a nude portrait of his famous admirer. (Unsurprisingly, the new Mrs Lugosi was less than impressed, and Clara was cited as 'the other woman' in divorce proceedings the following year.)

Listen to them. Children of the night. What music they make.

Looking at Lugosi today, it's hard to see what Clara Bow – who could have had her pick of the men of her day – saw in the macabre Hungarian actor. Charismatic? Certainly. Charming? Perhaps. But sexy…? The passage of time makes it all but impossible to view Bela in the same way audiences did in the 1920s and '30s – he has become so familiar to us as a camp icon that it has become difficult to take him as seriously as theatre and

Back to Thrill and Chill you!

SCREAMY!

SCARY!

TERRIFYING!

HORRIFIC!

WE'LL BE SCARING YOU—IF YOU DARE TO TAKE IT!

DRACULA
THE VAMPIRE BAT THAT LIVES ON HUMAN BLOOD!

STARRING
BELA LUGOSI

Goalart
RE-RELEASE

IMITATED BUT NEVER DUPLICATED!

filmgoers certainly did all those years ago.

One fan who can give an insight into his original magnetism is an actress we've already encountered, Carroll Borland, who played opposite Lugosi in the 1935 film *Mark of the Vampire*. *Mark of the Vampire* was the culmination of a lengthy fascination with Lugosi that had begun in her teens, while Carroll was still a drama student.

She submitted a script for a play entitled *Countess Dracula*; Bela expressed an interest in meeting the young writer, and Carroll became Lugosi's companion for a while, though she insists that their relationship remained platonic. Borland, who describes Bela himself as 'fascinating, intimidating, charming, exasperating, demanding and generous all at the same time', insists that the Hungarian will always be the definitive Dracula. 'When I say that Dracula is the creation of Lugosi, I do not mean to denigrate the contribution of Bram Stoker,' she said. 'But recall for a moment the description of Count Dracula in the Stoker novel. A seamed, revolting face. A hooked nose. A long, drooping moustache, and small, ember-lit eyes under craggy brows.

'But Dracula as embodied by Lugosi was suave, debonair, fascinating – from the sleek, smooth hair (the sign of the 'Latin lover' of the period) to the tip of his elegant opera pumps,' adds Carroll. 'And that face – so oddly divided. The Satanic widow's peak that pointed to the arrogant arch of the nose, the unexpected blue flame of the eyes, the dark circumflex of brows. And then the radically differing lower part of the face: the curved and pointing mouth above the provocatively oval chin, so deeply cleft. And isn't that the ultimate horror? Not the superficial fangs, the claws, the bloodied teeth – but the need to give oneself over to discover what dreadful consummation was achieved behind that merciful, concealing cloak? The modern films, for all their naïve explicitness, can never rival this.'

The passion Carroll brings to her description of her Gothic teen idol is contagious and helps explain just why Bela Lugosi's performance exerts such enduring power in the face of all the odds. He actually only played the role twice – the second time in one of the feeble Abbott and Costello comedy films Universal Studios used to try and squeeze the last few bucks out of their ailing horror franchises in the 1940s. Lugosi played several roles in which he is obviously Dracula in all but name – he was Count Mora in *Mark of the Vampire* – and was acclaimed for performances in other Universal pictures, playing a succession of mad scientists, hunchbacks and even the Frankenstein Monster. But he became typecast as a horror star early on, at a time when the genre was widely dismissed as trash. As the roles began to dry up, he suffered the humiliation of becoming Hollywood's first high-profile drug addict. Bela's last role was a posthumous cameo in *Plan 9 From Outer Space*, a 1959 sci-fi shocker oft-cited as the worst movie ever made.

'There are far worse things awaiting man than death.'

Furthermore, his most triumphant performance enjoys a mixed reputation, even among horror fans. Many aficionados criticise *Dracula* for being too talky and slow-moving, for looking too much like the original stage production, simply transferred to a Hollywood sound stage and filmed, with little thought given to the dynamic direction essential to good cinema. It's become fashionable to prefer the Spanish-language version, shot simultaneously on the same sets, with Carlos Villarías in the title role. Yet Villarías is no Lugosi, and if *Dracula* is a second-rate shocker, then it only serves to underline the power of Bela's truly iconic performance, one feature that lifted the film into the rarefied canon of Gothic immortality. Backstage onlookers report that Lugosi immersed himself in the role so completely – posing in front of mirrors intoning, 'I am Dracula' – that some wondered if he might have been a little mad. The Count consumed Lugosi. When he died he was buried in his infamous Dracula cape – the cloak that both made him famous, and doomed his Hollywood career.

'It is *women* who love horror,' the actor observed, ever insistent that there was an erotic component to the spell the vampire cast over his victim. 'Gloat over it. Feed on it. Are nourished by it. Shudder and cling and cry out – *but come back for more. Women have a predestination for suffering.* It is women who bear the race in bloody agony. Suffering is a kind of horror. Blood is a kind of horror. Therefore women are born with a predestination to horror in their very bloodstream. It is a biological thing.'

'I agree with the thesis that Count Dracula is a death figure,' pondered Carroll Borland, perhaps his greatest female fan, 'and that we all have a more or less hidden death wish. To many of us – women particularly – I think he stands for that great unknown factor. He is stronger than other men, more powerful, more feared. What a challenge, what a conquest! Women, who are the guardians and donors of the great life-force, see in him the dark enigma whom they can conquer only by being conquered.'

Afterword

As the cockerel crows and the dawning sun lifts the cloak of darkness, we reach the end of our exploration of the erotic, romantic realms of the undead. Confronted with the most sanguinary sex kittens and creepy Casanovas of the screen, we trust you have found some of your encounters intriguing, inspirational, hopefully even stimulating…

It is now time to take a moment to ponder, to wonder what light these creatures of the night might cast upon us, the viewers – for, without an audience, none of the diverse and exotic gallery of immortal bloodsuckers contained within these pages would ever have been conjured into existence. What is a predator without their prey – willing or otherwise? While vampires themselves cast no image in a mirror, they certainly seem to reflect some of the darkest secrets of the mortal libido.

The vampires of ancient lore were loathsome, putrid creatures who embodied the enigmas of death itself – specifically the amorphous threat posed by contagious disease before science began to reveal the invisible world of infection. The particular breed of undead that haunted our distant ancestors was primarily a plague demon. In most historical accounts, outbreaks of vampirism go hand-in-clammy-hand with the terrors of pestilence, of fatal epidemic diseases like tuberculosis. In modern mythology, particularly the potent myth-factories of film and fiction, the undead have evolved into sexual entities, just as sex and disease have become associated in our collective subconscious. Some have claimed that the Victorian author Bram Stoker, creator of the archetypal Hollywood bloodsucker Count Dracula, died of syphilis. A devastating sexually-transmitted disease, syphilis was an ominous nightmare that tainted the erotic fantasy lives of generations. A moment of ecstasy could open the gateway to both physical degeneration and spiritual damnation.

Numerous modern commentators have suggested links between contemporary vampire myth and the rise of AIDS – another contagion that creates a shadowy psychological linkage between sex, blood and death – first identified in 1981. 'The new blood culture is the bizarre pop by-product of a national obsession with all bodily fluids,' wrote Frank Rich in an article for the *New York Times*, inspired by the release of *Bram Stoker's Dracula* in 1992. 'It's a high-pitched, often hysterical acting out of the subliminal fantasies, both deadly and erotic, of a country that has awakened to the fact that the most insidious post-Cold War enemy is a virus.' Medical science has largely tamed syphilis, and while it is still struggling with AIDS, new apocalyptic threats such as international terrorism have eclipsed the disease as the principal panic troubling our collective sleep. Despite this, vampirism has not disappeared from our screens and bookshelves. Far from it – the past few years have witnessed a fresh invasion of bloodsuckers into our mass media.

Vampirism is an adaptable myth. Having evolved from demons of disease, the vampire is now a creature that feeds primarily upon our sexual anxieties, whatever they may be. Simultaneously, the zombie has emerged as a more effective carrier for our collective concerns over contagion (one more akin to the vampire of historical record), leaving his more cultivated undead cousin to embody less tangible fears. The modern vampire taps into unsettling psychological, emotional, even cultural territory – a chilling testament to the power of sexual desire to overwhelm us. Making us do things we truly shouldn't, it can overpower our better instincts, even our very identities. This is why the contemporary bloodsucker remains so very alluring. There is something in most of us that secretly rather likes the idea of becoming enslaved by lust, of surrendering, helpless, to the erotic pleasure instinct. Hence we have created vampires to mirror those we find sexually compelling, but believe we should resist – the forbidden fruit that tastes all the sweeter for being taboo, embodying pleasure illicit for a wide variety of reasons, ranging from the medical to the religious to the nationalistic.

Bela Lugosi claimed that it was his Hungarian nationality – specifically the thick, distinctive accent he established as the clichéd vocal characterisation of Dracula – that typecast him as a Hollywood villain. He wasn't alone. Having a foreign accent ensured that actors from England, Germany and Eastern Europe were routinely selected for such roles in American films (some might argue this stereotyping is still with us in modern Hollywood). According to writer Nina Auerbach, 'Dracula was not notably foreign until he became American.' In Stoker's original novel, once he reaches London, the Transylvanian Count strives with notable success to blend in. In Universal's *Dracula*, the vampire makes no attempt to conceal his Eastern-European identity. Some reports suggest that Lugosi was cast in the title role because studio executives thought the Hungarian looked swarthy and unsavoury – unsettlingly foreign, even alien. However, while Bela's Count caused many viewers' flesh to creep, others like actress Clara Bow found this sinister stranger curiously magnetic.

The classic black-and-white Hollywood horror movies of the 1930s were largely made by European ex-pats, both in front of and behind the camera, with American actors taking the roles of wholesome heroes and heroines. But it is the monsters we remember, and among the sundry mummies and wolfmen, only Dracula can claim to have been suave or debonair. For a plethora of reasons, early twentieth-century Americans were justifiably suspicious of the 'Old World' of Europe, their mistrust reinforced by the events of the First World War. In 1917 the US was dragged into the bloody slaughter, resulting in the loss of well over 100,000 American lives in a conflict many patriots felt was none of their business. Many sceptical US citizens felt much the same about being drawn into the Second World War in 1941, as fresh rivers of American blood were spilled on distant battlefields.

There is a strong isolationist tradition in American culture and politics, a feeling that the Old World, far across the Atlantic Ocean, remains hopelessly dissolute and corrupt, a place of immoral aristocracies and impure pleasures best left to its own devices. It's a tradition early Hollywood horror films traded upon profitably. But it's also an ambivalent one. While upstanding US citizens might piously condemn the benighted Old World as outmoded and decadent in comparison to their wholesome, progressive homeland, there was still a guilty tendency in the American psyche to secretly find the corruption and decadence a source of uncomfortable fascination, particularly when embodied in the saturnine form of a vampire. With Count Dracula and his disciples, Hollywood thrilled audiences with the forbidden fantasy of the effete, aristocratic foreign lover, safely despatched by manly, democratic, home-grown heroes on screen, but lingering on in the imagination long after the lights went up.

Of course, by this time the Old World was making horror films of its own, and while these weren't devoid of the xenophobic overtones of their Hollywood equivalents, they often exploited different attitudes and prejudices when conjuring up their particular manifestations of forbidden desire. Unlike any other studio, England's Hammer Films has become synonymous with the vampire. Exactly how much Hammer's most famous vampire, Count Dracula as played by Christopher Lee, has in common with that other quintessential cinematic sex symbol, Sean Connery as James Bond, has already been noted. But while Bond was a very British hero, Dracula, of course, was a villain, played by an actor, incidentally, who had previously struggled to find work because he looked 'too foreign'. Significantly, while 007 was a thoroughly modern character, with all of his hi-tech gadgetry, the immortal Count in his crumbling medieval castle personified the long-lost past. Curiously, Hammer's reign as the world's leading specialists in Gothic horror, from the late '50s to the mid-'70s, coincided with a time when Victoriana was hardly in vogue. Sinking to an all-time low, the era has never been less fashionable in British culture.

'Gothic' was originally a dismissive term for medieval architecture and culture, long condemned as dark and barbaric. It was reclaimed by authors and architects in the late 1700s and early 1800s. Reviving the aesthetics of the era, they rediscovered and reinvented the Middle Ages as an era of evocative drama and thrilling mystery. This led directly to the atmospheric neo-Gothic architecture of the Victorian era and, of course, Gothic literature like Bram Stoker's 1897 novel *Dracula*. By the 1950s, Victorian style had fallen out of fashion, widely reviled as vulgar and sentimental. Victorian antiques fell even further out of vogue in the 1960s – associated with outmoded imperialist ideologies and repressive moral values – as the sexual revolution gained pace and youth culture railed against tradition and authority in all its forms. Ironically, it was in this environment that Hammer studios launched their series of Gothic horror films, almost all of which were set in the Victorian era. They were not only successful, but enjoyed particular popularity among younger audiences.

Looking back, Hammer's distinctive look actively defied the fashions of the era. While skinny catwalk models like Twiggy were making boyish figures all the rage, Hammer hunted for voluptuous starlets with curvaceous feminine figures and long locks, in contrast to the bobbed hair then in vogue. While feminists were adopting unisex attire or burning their bras, Hammer's costume departments were outfitting their actresses with cleavage-enhancing corsets. It's most unlikely that the studio was deliberately bucking such trends, but the reason their films struck such a chord may have had everything to do with offering a fantasy world on screen that contrasted so strongly with what audiences were supposed to find 'attractive' or 'exciting'. Significantly, Christopher Lee's Count first truly falters in *Dracula A.D. 1972*, Hammer's ill-fated attempt to bring their Gothic franchise up-to-date with hipster culture. The film is a guilty pleasure today; a cringe-inducing illustration of just how cool the mock-Victorian style of the studio's Gothic classics appear when placed in painful juxtaposition with contemporary fashion.

Hammer studios were, of course, above all a business, producing films to make money rather than political statements. If there was any morality implicit in their films, it was about the triumph of good over evil, of the status quo over creeping deviance – scarcely a subversive message. Few studios can have made as frequent use of the crucifix – the symbol of Christian authority – as Hammer did in their horror films. Yet, whatever the scriptwriters and directors may have intended, audiences responded more powerfully to the villains of these films, most notably Christopher Lee's Satanic Count, who became a surprise sex symbol on the back of *The Horror of Dracula* in 1958. Some critics have even gone so far as to reinterpret Hammer's first vampire film, casting Lee's Dracula as the hero of the picture and Peter Cushing's hawkish Van Helsing as its villain. According to this interpretation, the vampire-hunters infiltrate Castle Dracula with murderous intent and a plan to stake the Count's undead bride, inspiring a justly angry Dracula to retaliate, attempting to claim one of their brides as a replacement. The mortal womenfolk appear notably enthusiastic at the prospect.

Even if this isn't what director Terence Fisher or scriptwriter Jimmy Sangster originally intended, it's a radical reading of *The Horror of Dracula* that stands up to scrutiny. Similar analyses can be applied to most of Hammer's vampire pictures. Where vampirism represents sexual anarchy in opposition to staid domestic bliss, it's no surprise to find many of the audience members quietly rooting for the erotic anarchists over their popcorn. Frank Langella's 1979 *Dracula* made this thread even more overt, a film Nina Auerbach praises as a feminist-friendly version of the story in her book *Our Vampires, Ourselves*: 'In this breathtaking if confusing movie, Stoker's good men are villains; Stoker's vampire is hero; the women, victims no more, embrace vampirism with rapture as the sole available escape from patriarchy [...] Evolving from the self-imprisoned Bela Lugosi to the Promethean Frank Langella, Dracula progresses from death-bringing foreigner to angelic harbinger of better times. But as he casts off crypt and coffin for erotic enlightenment, he looks to the past, not the future...'

One taboo area Hammer explored with enthusiasm in the 1970s was lesbianism. While not the first to equate vampirism with Sapphic lust, it was the British studio who established it as an erotic sub-genre of vampire cinema with their 'Karnstein Trilogy'. Needless to say, few feminist film historians are impressed by Hammer's forays into the realms of homoeroticism and many mainstream critics regard the films as crudely exploitative. But they did help demonstrate that audiences could find lesbian love a turn-on on the big screen – at least if draped in the Gothic trappings of a period horror. One might argue that Anne Rice did the same for male homosexuality with her 1976 novel *Interview with the Vampire*, as manifest in the erotically charged scenes played out by two of Hollywood's most bankable stars in the 1994 film version. (Eleven years before *Brokeback Mountain* supposedly blazed new trails with its depiction of the love affair between two cowboys, played by Heath Ledger and Jake Gyllenhaal.)

If the vampire embodies illicit love, then the minute that expression of the taboo desire becomes socially acceptable, the vampire must evolve or risk becoming toothless. This is a large part of the reason so many vampire aficionados reacted badly to Stephenie Meyer's *Twilight Saga* and the subsequent film adaptations. In the twenty-first century, it looked like the undead had quite literally lost their fangs. Meyer's creatures of the night had transformed from deliciously dark embodiments of forbidden desire into walking warnings against sex out of wedlock. Worse still, Edward Cullen, the principle vampire love interest, is complicit in this message, an undead posterboy for the abstinence movement.

Yet you could argue that, in focusing on the erotic anticipation of lust deferred, *Twilight* has successfully uncovered an unspoken modern sexual taboo. In our age of increasingly commodified sexuality, is a high-school student who gets off on abstinence a more radical interpretation than foreign vampires, Victorian vampires, libertine vampires, or even gay vampires?

Of course, that's wide open to debate and contemporary social tensions lend extra friction to such discussion. Supporting pre-marital celibacy scarcely makes Stephenie Meyer a subversive, particularly when powerful reactionary political and religious authorities are singing – almost literally – from the same hymn sheet. Exasperated opponents of abstinence campaigns argue that, far from reducing such problems, this reactionary approach appears to encourage unwanted pregnancies and STDs among the young. As Robert Pattinson, the actor who portrays Edward in *Twilight*, observes, 'The book is based on the virtues of chastity, but I think it has the opposite effect on its readers.' Others object to the reactionary tone of the books. Authoress Laurell K. Hamilton accuses Meyer of sanitising the genre, taking strong exception to the heroine's characterization as a passive, virginal princess: 'The fact that women are so attracted to that idea – that they want to wait for Prince Charming rather than taking control of their own life – I find that frightening.'

Hamilton lays claim to having pioneered the paranormal vampire romance genre, most notably with her best-selling Anita Blake novels, beginning with *Guilty Pleasures* in 1993. In contrast to *Twilight*, these are unabashedly erotic books, with no shortage of explicit sex – little of it within the bounds of holy wedlock. A TV movie adaptation of Hamilton's Anita Blake character is scheduled to air in late 2010 at the time of writing.

The decision to bring Anita's sexy saga to the screen no doubt has something to do with the success of *True Blood*, the TV series taken from the similarly steamy *Southern Vampire Mysteries*, penned by Hamilton's fellow vampire romance novelist Charlaine Harris. As interpreted by Alan Ball (best known for the award-winning funereal drama series *Six Feet Under*), *True Blood* invokes many of the vampire archetypes touched upon above – shying away from none of the old questions of racism and xenophobia – as well as boasting an undead hero who represents the arcane allure of the past in contrast with the brash cynicism of the modern world.

Perhaps *True Blood*'s boldest innovation is in casting vampires as potential victims. Vampire blood is a powerful narcotic with aphrodisiac properties if ingested by mortals; hence we're presented with people preying upon vampires, turning the tables by drinking from the bloodsuckers. The storyline where human characters Jason and Amy kidnap a personable vampire named Eddie, in order to milk him for blood, is one of the most unsettling in the first series.

Yet this idea of turning the tables on the familiar vampire myth is nothing new. In his 1954 novel, *I Am Legend*, author Richard Matheson envisages a world where human society is overrun by a vampire plague. The twist in the tale comes when lonely survivor Richard Neville appreciates that, as the stealthy, solitary figure coming out of hiding only to slay members of the newly evolved vampire society in their beds, he has become the monster. (The book's clever message is almost wholly ignored in the feather-brained 2007 big-screen adaptation starring Will Smith.)

Numerous studies of screen vampires have served notice on our culture's favourite supernatural predators over the years, convinced that every conceivable aspect of the myth has literally been done to death. All such obituaries have, of course, proven premature. The vampire remains in rude health, with numerous forthcoming film and TV projects announced for upcoming release at the time of writing. Doubtless, the market will reach saturation point and the crimson tide of screen vampires will once more diminish to a scarlet trickle. Yet it will equally doubtless continue; deepening to become a flood once again as soon as the next novelist or screenwriter finds a fresh way of exploring our fascination with cinema's sexiest myth. So long as we remain curious about the darker fringes of our own libidos, enthralled by the intoxicating moments where sex and death embrace, vampires will continue to evolve and to adapt to satisfy that craving. Leaving us with the question – who feeds upon who?